Updated and Revised

*Instructions for car parking, bus routes,
safety, what to wear*

'Leads you thoughtfully and carefully step-by-step along the
entire route, and positively sparkles with local lore.' *Lifetimes*

'With this guide you can't fail to enjoy yourself ... particularly
good on foolproof directions.' *Ireland of the Welcomes*

'[J.B. Malone] has introduced generations of walkers to the
delights of Wicklow and is reputed to be on first-name terms
with each and every rock in the county ... this account has
everything.' *Irish Mountain Log*

'He designed the Wicklow Way. He of all people is an authority
on the Way ... his description is full of anecdote and comment.'
David Rowe, An Taisce Journal

'Should be grabbed from the bookshelves as soon as possible ...
a must buy.' *Irish Independent*

*With this book you and your family
can join the Way at many points,
and enjoy Wicklow –*

'the garden of Ireland'

The Wicklow Way

The famous Wicklow Way, Ireland's favourite walkers' trail, was planned and laid out by J.B. Malone, working with Cospoir.

Inevitably, the Way has undergone alteration over the years. A previous edition of this book incorporated revisions made by J.B.Malone himself before his death. Since then, other changes to the Way have occurred, and this edition of the book has been updated by Jean Boydell, inspector of waymarked ways for the National Waymarked Ways Committee.

The publishers wish to thank the National Waymarked Ways Committee (whose work was formerly carried out by Cospoir) for their co-operation in keeping this book up-to-date.

THE COMPLETE
Wicklow Way
A STEP-BY-STEP GUIDE
(revised edition)

BY

J.B. MALONE

Updated by

JEAN BOYDELL

With an Introduction by

JAMES PLUNKETT

THE O'BRIEN PRESS
DUBLIN

First published 1988 by
The O'Brien Press Ltd.
20 Victoria Road, Dublin 6, Ireland.
Revised edition published 1990.
Updated and revised 1993, 1997.

British Library Cataloguing in Publication Data.

Malone, J.B.
The complete Wicklow Way: a step-by-step guide
1. Wicklow (County) Recreations: Walking – Visitors' Guides
I Title
796.55'1'094184

ISBN 0-86278-158-2

10 9 8 7 6 5

Typesetting, design and layout: The O'Brien Press Ltd.
Cover separations: Lithoset Ltd.
Printing: Guernsey Press Ltd.

Front cover photograph: Lough Bray, Co Wicklow, courtesy of Bord Fáilte.
Back cover photograph: round tower and monastic ruins, Glendalough, Co
Wicklow, courtesy of Bord Fáilte.

By the same author:

'Over the Hills' Series *(Evening Herald)* 1938-1975.

The Open Road (Independent Newspapers) 1950.

Walking in Wicklow (Helicon, Dublin) 1964.

Know Your Dublin (in collaboration with Liam C. Martin)
(Sceptre Books, Dublin) 1968.

A Word of Thanks
from J.B. Malone

Neither this book, nor the Wicklow Way itself, could have been
set up without the help of my wife, and of
my friends and colleagues in Cospoir [whose work is now
carried out by the National Waymarked Ways Committee].
Especially I have to thank Larry Scally, Michael Gallagher and
Bill Condon for making so many journeys on my behalf, while
on the research side I must acknowledge the unfailing help of
the Director and staff of the National Library.

Route Sketch Abbrevations

Wire Fence	*Wf*	Ride Line	*R.L.*
Wooden (fence) Posts	*W*	Sign Post	*S.P.*
Wooden Gate	*W.g.*	Footbridge	*F.B.*
Iron Gate	*I.g.*	Townland	*TLd*
Stone Wall	*S.W.*	Viewpoint	*V*
Parking	**P**		

How To Use This Book

1

The Wicklow Way is divided here into seven single-day sections. The complete Way can thus be done by fit and experienced walkers in one week's walking.

2

The less dedicated can choose a journey to suit them from the Shorter Walks, selecting a trip on a time basis (all walks are timed in this guide), or a trip that gives the flavour of this splendidly varied countryside.

The Shorter Walks include circular walks, planned for motorists, based on convenient car parks, and any section of the Way included in a shorter walk has cross-references to the route sketches for the main route.

Alternatively, you might choose simply to walk part of a day-long walk (the main sections of this book) and return by the same route.

3

Sections of any shorter walk that are not on the Wicklow Way, give National Grid six-figure references for all landmarks; the use of the grid is fully explained on the margins of the Ordnance Survey maps Discovery Series Sheets 50, 56 and 62 which show the Wicklow Way.

Dedication
To my wife, Peg, who made this book possible
and
To the memory of Dr J. F. Cronin

Contents

Introduction to the First Edition

James Plunkett

J.B. Malone tells us that he started hill walking in 1931 with a trip to the Hell Fire Club on Mountpelier Hill. It is a coincidence that I too began a lifelong love affair with the hidden ways of the Dublin and Wicklow mountains in that same year. I was eleven at the time and we were camping above the old military barracks (then referred to as The Reformatory) in Glencree. We arrived in darkness and the next morning I woke before the others and crept to the door of the tent to see where we were. What I found ranged about me was so beautiful it almost stopped my breath: dew on the grass; a rabbit scampered away; the mountainside sloping down to the valley below; the river flowing through it with the sun on its golden brown waters; bogland and the grey boulders scattered in the stream; Kippure with its shining crown of mist and its slopes all agleam with morning sunlight; the landscape around all granite and greenery, all purples and browns. I was enslaved forever.

J.B.'s corresponding enthusiasm became known to me through his first series on the byways of Wicklow in the *Evening Herald* in the late thirties and his first book *The Open Road* published in 1950, a copy of which (though much bedraggled by the wear and tear of time) I still have. And then, in 1962, I met him personally.

The occasion was a discussion on the possibility of a series of walks for screening on RTE Television which had just been set up. The title selected was 'Mountain and Meadow'. It ran during the summer of 1962 and covered several of the Co. Wicklow routes. In 1963 it spread out generally with similar walks in various counties. Throughout both series I found J.B. amiable, knowledgeable, and a generous imparter of information from his familiarity with the apparently inexhaustible lore that time had attached to the fields and hills of Ireland.

In 1980 I had the pleasure of his company again. J.B. had become Field Officer for the Cospoir's Long Distance Walks Committee and had been developing a scheme for a 'Wicklow Way'. The idea was an attractive one and RTE decided to make a one-hour film about it. It was like old times again, except that now we had the benefits of colour and enormously improved technology. It proved `immensely popular with audiences and gave J.B. the opportunity once again to make use of his deep knowledge of the countryside and his ability to impart information on each and every thing the countryside could present. For me the opportunity of travelling in his agreeable company once again assuaged the now noticeable toll that high hills were beginning to exact from ageing limbs. It seemed as nothing to the hard J.B. himself, who is recorded as saying: 'Walking has been my way of life. It was through walking I met my wife and by my walking articles I reared my family.'

What follows is part of the fruit of that love.

James Plunkett
1988

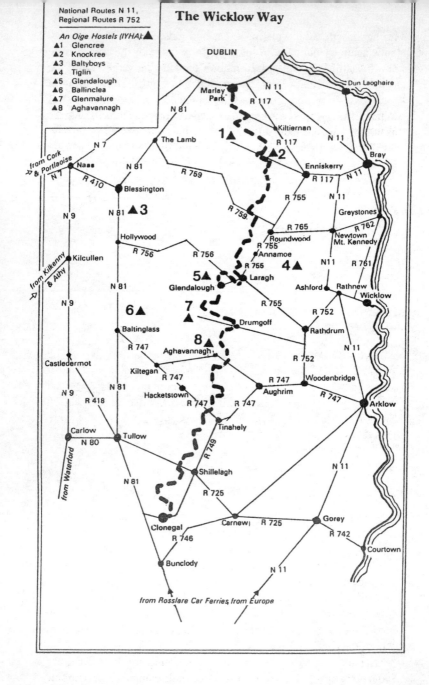

The Wicklow Way

National Routes N 11,
Regional Routes R 752

An Oige Hostels (IYHA):▲
▲1 Glencree
▲2 Knockree
▲3 Baltyboys
▲4 Tiglin
▲5 Glendalough
▲6 Ballinclea
▲7 Glenmalure
▲8 Aghavannagh

Tackling the Wicklow Way

When I first worked out and published my original scheme for the Wicklow Way, in 1966, I little thought that some twelve years later a semi-state body, Cospoir (The National Sports Council), would be active in implementing the idea – and paying me to do it!

Some changes were made, of course, to my first ideas. The Way, instead of returning to Dublin via West Wicklow as originally planned, pushed on south to Clonegal in Co. Carlow, for Cospoir were already thinking in terms of a national network of tracks and paths to cover all Ireland.

Other changes were made, since the Cospoir Committee, having no compulsory powers, were very occasionally refused a way-leave, while new forest roads and some forest extensions altered things elsewhere. But by and large, the route remains substantially as planned in 1966.

The Wicklow Way follows a NE-SW course, from Marlay Park, Rathfarnham, Dublin 14, to Clonegal, Co. Carlow (131km), rising from 80m above sea level to 630m, before ending about 60m. It keeps mainly to the east flanks of the mountains and it does not cross summits unless a path already does so. South of Aghavannagh the Way passes west of the ranges for most of the rest of the route into Clonegal.

The Marking System

The Wicklow Way is marked by square black posts, displaying yellow arrowheads, horizontal at a turning, vertical for straight on and often the yellow "walking man" symbol. Partly on grounds of expense, and partly for conservation, the system of minimal marking has been used, so markers are set only at junctions, or where there is about 500km between junctions – instead of the system, sometimes used on the Continent, of setting markers at 30m intervals. On straight sections without junctions, markers are at 500m intervals. Road signs have also been used in many places where the route meets a road.

On parts of the Way, in soft mountain ground, markers have been loosened or pushed over by grazing animals using them as rubbing posts; they have been split by frost or uprooted by heavy machinery during timber felling, and there has been deliberate vandalism, such as blanking out direction arrows with mud or hacking them off with axes, as well as breaking off signpost arms.

But this book is written to help you to navigate the Way, with or without the markers, from Marlay to Clonegal.

Nature and the Way

Geology

The Wicklow mountains are the largest unbroken block of high ground in Ireland, covering almost the same area as the massif of Mont Blanc, being about 50km long by 40km wide.

About six times as old as the upstart Alps or the aspiring Himalayas, these mountains began perhaps five hundred million years ago when, in a shallow sea, sediments were laid down, that long after became the purple Cambrian rock, around Bray and the Sugar Loaves, rock which was later uplifted to link Wicklow with north Wales. Then during the next hundred million years further sediments became the Ordovician rocks which once covered all Wicklow and Wexford, and most of Kildare and Carlow besides.

The next stage began with a mighty upsurge of molten granite which baked and altered the rocks, in a broad belt on either side of the fiery mass, turning the Ordovician rocks into sparkling mica schists. The granite cooled, to form a lopsided dome, steeper on the east side, 43km long, 32km across at the widest, itself only the crest of the largest granite batholith in the British Isles. From this dome and its mica-schist fringes, three hundred million years of weathering, the relentless assault of ice, and sometimes the encroaching sea, have combined to produce the mountains as we know them. In this unfinished geologic story, the midget hand of man has played the smallest part, with the scars of his tiny quarries and mines, with the re-establishment of an Ice Age lake for a reservoir, or the siting of a pump-storage hydro-electric scheme or a TV mast, on a mountain top.

Wicklow's state forests are affected by the rocks beneath them like any other plant. A forestry man once showed me two Douglas fir trees, planted the same day, reared from the same batch of seed – one towered sixty feet high, the other had barely made six feet of growth in the same time. One tree must have rooted in a pocket of good soil, the other met a rocky obstacle and had only minimum soil to draw on.

Tree growth is faster in Ireland than in many countries from which our trees come originally, because here we do not have prolonged winter frosts, so growth may go on the whole year round.

It is fashionable among conservationists to denounce the forest service for insensitive planting of our hills with 'monotonous conifers' instead of native hardwood trees (oak, beech, birch and ash). There has been improvement in this regard in recent years. Quite a few forests are now edged with beech and birch trees, while modern methods of timber extraction open up our forests rapidly, revealing distant views, and giving the appearance of natural woodland.

As a walker, I feel we have gained greatly from state forestry, not only by new picnic and parking sites, but above all by the wealth of forest roads, tracks on firebreaks, paths on ridelines, giving easier access to the higher tops.

Plant and Animal Life

The underlying rocks control the plant life in the Wicklow mountain landscape, with sedges and the delicate, white-topped bog cotton on the compact granite grounds; but heather, furze, and fern favour the better-drained mica-schist borders, like the Cambrian rocks around Bray and the Sugar Loaf Mountains.

Plant life in turn influences animal life, but which animals you will see on the Way depends on the size and quietness of your party, while, if you take a dog along, no animal life at all is likely to appear!

The wild deer of Wicklow that you may glimpse are now the offspring of mating between the native Irish Red and the Japanese or Sika deer, first imported by the Powerscourt Estate, about a century ago.

The pure Irish Red deer unfortunately seems to be extinct in

Wicklow now, though there is a record of a fourteen-pointer Red shot near Laragh around 1930.

In contrast, the Sika deer are flourishing all along the trail, almost from the gates of Marlay Park to Clonegal, but most travellers will only hear the short whistling alarm call of the Sika or catch a glimpse of the white backside of the animal dashing off through trees – these white patches are themselves an alarm signal, a sort of undercoat, revealed only in panic flight. My most dramatic sighting of Sika deer was where the Wicklow Way meets the Military Road (Sketch 24).

I was facing Laragh when a solitary Sika, with a tremendous bound, cleared the forest fence and the road ditch on my left, landed on the road, turned her graceful head to look at me, didn't like what she saw, then from a standing start soared away over the ditch and forest fence to the right.

Foxes are less often met on the Way since the rabbits, their main food, were cut down by 'the myxo', as the rabbit-killing disease myxomatosis was familiarly called, and since dustbin collections were begun in counties Dublin and Wicklow. Like a good soldier, the fox is a first-class forager, and takes the line of least resistance – why scour the high mountains for scanty prey when down in the lowlands there are fat black refuse sacks bulging with succulent household left-overs?

Weather

One aspect of nature that parties of any and every size can enjoy is the unending drama of weather, the factor that makes any day on the Way a unique day, that will never be exactly repeated, with a cloud shadow resting on that particular forest patch, a wisp of mist drifting over that summit beyond the lough, factors that sum up for me the whole enticement and charm of mountain walking.

The wind on the Wicklow Way can range from a gentle breeze that barely stirs the fern fronds, to a howling gale that almost makes you crawl on all fours. I recall a strange effect one time in West Wicklow (not on the Way), when coming down from Church Mountain on a calm, autumn evening. Ahead of me, across a deep, heather-clad glen, rose part of the hill known as the Corriebracks, and quite suddenly the whole scene ahead seemed to quiver, as if a giant hand had stroked the mountain slopes. A wind from nowhere ruffled the heather and a purple mist of pollen rose up, hung in the air less than half a minute, and was gone without trace before even a breath of air reached me.

Like all large mountain groups, the Wicklow summits make their own weather. This is fairly often seen on the Wicklow Way, when a steady, visible, westerly air stream starts to rise and fall as it passes over the tops and the glens, till the air wave begins to resemble the graph of world trade deficits. Each air wave crest is marked by a cigar-shaped cloud, each trough by blue sky. *Lenticular-cumulus* is the official name of this cloud, called 'lent-cu' by air pilots and hang gliders. This has a special importance for camera users on the Wicklow Way, because if you are in the shadow of one of these cigar-shaped clouds, there you will stay, as the 'lent-cu' does not move with the wind, but remains perched on each crest of the air-wave until conditions change, building up to windward, decaying on the leeward side.

There are strange sounds to be heard in these hills, such as those my wife and I heard once, when seated on the summit of Tonelagee, the third-highest top in Wicklow (817m). The air suddenly got colder and, turning round to look west, we saw a vicious, inky-black squall heading straight for us. Huddled down under capes and anoraks, we had driving hail for less than three minutes, then the wind dropped and we heard a sound, swelling to a loud drum-roll. It was the rattle of countless hailstones striking the calm surface of Lough Ouler far below the summit and cradled under the cliffs from which this mountain is named – 'backside to the wind' (*tón le gaoith*).

Accidents

If a person in a group suffers injury, one member of the party should go to the nearest road for help, or to one of the parking places (marked P on the maps in this book and on the O.S. maps Sheets 50, 56 and 62 1/50000). Meanwhile the injured person should be protected from hypothermia ('wind-chill'), a fatal loss of bodyheat. Other members should contribute spare pullovers, etc. A 'space-blanket' (just a large plastic sheet) is ideal for wrapping around the injured person or, failing that, the largest available plastic bag, to preserve vital heat.

Exhaustion can also cause hypothermia, so don't rush out to do the entire Way in a day, but start small, gradually widening your experience and building up fitness. (I admit I haven't always kept to this good rule myself!)

Common sense reminds beginners and experienced walkers alike that the Wicklow Way traverses part of the largest unbroken block of mountains in Ireland, which, like most Irish upland areas, sees few walkers. Often no other travellers are met on the Way, except near Dublin. Hence a minor injury, a slight sprain, could leave you lying a week on the trail before help arrives.

Also remember that the weather is even less trustworthy than many politicians. My log-books record three out of every five days as 'bad', which means rain, wind, and low cloud on the hills.

Rain gear is essential, but really waterproof and wind-proof anoraks tend to be expensive although there are cheaper ones available which offer reasonable protection. An anorak should have a hood.

Boots are better than shoes on the Way. They should be a half-size larger than your normal shoes, as two pairs of socks should be worn (one light, one heavy wool pair).

Food can be bought along the Way at the following centres:

Enniskerry (4.5km E of the trail)	
Roundwood (2.5km E)	
Annamoe (2km E)	
Laragh (on trail)	
Askanagap (2.5km NNE)	[limited supplies]
Knockananna (3km W)	
Tinahely (2km E)	
Mullinacuff (on trail)	[limited supplies]
Shillelagh (3km E)	
Clonegal (on trail).	

All equipment should be stowed so that both hands are free (for balance and for comfort). The answer is to have a jacket with big pockets, or else a medium-sized rucksack, not one of the monster packs designed for a month in the Himalayas.

A rucksack can be cheaply and easily 'waterproofed', by lining it with an ordinary plastic refuse sack, thus keeping your gear snug and dry. For further security, items like spare socks, sleeping gear etc can be put into their own plastic bags.

Short-distance Walkers

Short-distance walkers should study the maps in this book dealing with the area they are about to traverse and judge for themselves what equipment they will need. It is, of course, always better to err on the side of caution.

Families with young children, intending to make short strolls on the Wicklow Way, obviously do not need all the equipment listed above but the essentials are still the same – rain gear, strong footwear, torch, whistle and small first-aid kit.

With children, because they expend far more energy than adults, some simple food that quickly restores the blood sugar is a good idea, such as raisins or oranges or boiled sweets.

Remember that the legend of the 'hungry grass' (*féar gortach*), widespread in Ireland, applies particularly in Wicklow, where a whole section (not on the Way), is called the Faragurtha Mountains.

The 'hungry grass' looks exactly like any other grass, but when you step on it, down you go with sudden weakness and hunger.

Tradition declares that the grass grows where a famine victim died, or where a coffin rested during a mountain funeral. The traditional cure is a mouthful of currany bread (sugar again!).

Modern science says that heavy exercise above 300m can reduce the blood-sugar count, leading to something like a diabetic coma, so parents may note that there is something in the old hungry grass idea, after all.

Finally, walkers on the Way should follow the three DON'Ts of Irish walking

1 DON'T wear denim jeans on the hill. Once they are wet, they give absolutely no protection from wind-chill, leading to fatal hypothermia. Wear heavier, warmer pants.
2 DON'T bring dogs on the Way, for Wicklow is predominantly sheep country. Sheep owners are now legally entitled to shoot any dog seen rambling loose near their flocks.
3 DON'T light any fire within 1km of any wood or plantation (it's illegal!) and make sure that ALL fires, anywhere, likewise matches and cigarette ends, are OUT before you move on. In this way, you help to KEEP IRELAND GREEN.

Changes on the Way

The rate of change has stepped up in Wicklow, as everywhere else. On a trail the length of the Wicklow Way, it is hard to be sure that every new landmark, every new forest, forest road junction, new building, new radio mast or new monument is mentioned. Felled forest, changes in forest roads, broken stiles or bridges, etc, may also lead to changes to the description of the route. In addition, the route itself may also be changed for various reasons although the policy of the National Waymarked Ways Committee is to keep this to a minimum. The co-operation of walkers will be welcomed to keep this trail guide as up-to-date as possible.

Equipment and Precautions

Like any other mountain walk, following the Wicklow Way requires certain basic equipment and some common-sense care.

Long-distance Walkers

Long-distance walkers who intend to spend complete days in the mountains should regard the following as basic equipment:

Map, strong footwear (preferably boots but not necessarily heavy boots), compass, torch, whistle, food, wind-proof and rain-proof clothing, basic first-aid kit.

You should know how to use map and compass – instruction is available from An Oige (Irish Youth Hostel Association), or on courses in mountain navigation run by the National Adventure Centre at Tiglin near Roundwood and in the leading walking clubs.

Torch and whistle are essential, as the International Mountain Distress Signal is six long whistle blasts per minute (by day), six torch flashes per minute (at night) – repeated till help arrives.

Strollers, Cars and Families

The Wicklow Way is designed not only for experienced hill walkers but also for beginners in rambling, and for the family that does not want to walk for more than an hour and a half, or two hours at most, from their car. Since the Way is one long continuous route you do not after each day's walk end up back at your car. You may decide, for a shorter walk, simply to go as far along the route as you wish, then double back to your car, getting the views from the other side on your return journey. If however you want to do a circular walk you should consult the Shorter Walks sections of each day's walking.

Most Dublin-based walking clubs drive to their starting points, though this does sometimes present a problem, especially if, like most people, you wish to return to your starting point by a different route.

The solutions to the car problem are usually either to have a non-walking driver who will be waiting for you at a parking place further along the trail, or else to use two cars, one being placed at the intended finish of the walk, after which the party travels back to the start of the walk.

Obviously this 'car-ferry' or 'two-car trick' does not work well with a big party, where at the end of the day the five or six drivers have to be ferried back to the original start, while their passengers wait as patiently as possible on the roadside, getting gradually chilled, in some shelterless spot, about nine miles from nowhere.

Wherever or however you park, please do so with consideration for others. NEVER park so that you block a field gate. Even if the gate looks as if it has not been opened since Adam was in the Highlanders, this may be the day that the vet calls to tend a sick animal in the field, or a tillage contractor arrives with heavy machinery.

Equally important, cars must NEVER block a state forest entrance, with or without a barrier, as at any time fire engines may have to go in, and even at weekends timber contractors may have to bring trucks and machinery in or out.

If forest gates and barriers are open, resist the temptation to drive in and get up to the Way without effort. Some forest roads are guaranteed to rip the sump out of any family car. Rounding a corner, you may find, as I did once, the whole road completely covered with a 'raft' of giant logs left by contractors intending to resume work early on Monday.

On weekdays, a forest entrance left open means that some work is going on, maybe miles from the Wicklow Way, in another part of the forest, and there is a good chance that you and your family could be locked in for the night, if not for the weekend, when forest workers depart about 4.30 p.m.

Wherever you park, remember to leave no valuables on the seats or elsewhere in your car, as robberies from parked cars are not unknown in Irish mountain areas. Once, when a friend and I parked (in midweek) at a large, well-known forest car park, we returned to find that we had been robbed. The car had been placed at the very back of the parking place, almost out of sight of the road – don't make things too easy for thieves!

Maps for the Way

In this 'step by step' guide to the Wicklow Way, you have a diagram showing how the route relates to Leinster generally, then there are diagrams showing the ground covered on each day's trip, and a series of route sketches, covering the trail in detail, showing tarmac roads, forest roads, tracks, paths, stiles, gates, forest barriers, and car parks.

For motorists with young families, or for holiday-makers staying at a hostel or hotel near the route, the diagrams and sketches in this book allow you to select a trip, long or short as you please. The route sketches show the actual line of the trail by heavy black arrows, double-headed, so that the Way can be followed towards Marlay, or towards Clonegal, as preferred. All your requirements on or near the Way should be thoroughly catered for by these maps.

Beyond the line of the Wicklow Way, if you want to know what a certain distant landmark is, or where you can get refreshment or accommodation, the area is shown on the Ordnance Survey Discovery Series 1/50000 maps Sheets 50, 56 and 62. The Ordnance Survey 1/50000 scale 'Wicklow Way' sheet, the first recreational map issued in this part of Ireland, is no longer available. The Discovery Series maps are a big improvement, not least since their contours are metric, with 50m contour lines, whereas the heights and contours on the older maps were not metric, and there was a damnable 'jump' from 100 feet interval to 250 feet on the contours above 1,000 feet! This gave a deceptively smooth outline to the upper slopes of the higher hills in Wicklow – you would often discover that the climb was much stiffer than you had anticipated. A map guide to the Wicklow Way (1/50000 scale) is also available.

For a general view of the whole Way, see the O.S. 'Holiday Map' Series, Sheet 3, scale 1/250000, almost four miles to one inch, and Messrs Bartholomew's 'Dublin-Athlone' Sheet of their 'Quarter

Inch' map. Also, there are map boards detailing the route set up at Marlay (north car park), Curtlestown Forest entrance, Crone Forest, The Pier Gates, Laragh, Drumgoff, Iron Bridge and in Clonegal village (on the green). There is also an information display board for the Wicklow Way at Marlay (south car park).

In this book I will provide, where relevant, grid references to Ordnance Survey maps, indicated as follows: (O 148 255).

A special 1/25000 map of Glendalough area (showing the Way as far as Glenmalure) is available in the Visitors' Centre, Glendalough, or from the National Parks and Wildlife Service, 51 St Stephen's Green, Dublin 2.

Walkers without Maps

Anyone with a sense of history soon feels the long centuries behind Wicklow's landscape, but across these hills have marched many figures who left no trace of their passage, save perhaps an obscure placename, a bit of folklore, or some forgotten volumes in a dusty library. A gentleman with the almost too appropriate name of J.B. Trotter seems to have been the first to walk for pleasure in Wicklow, or at least the first to record his journeys, in his *Walks in Ireland ... 1812-1817 ... in a series of letters*. This Mr Trotter was known to his contemporaries as 'the unfortunate Trotter' from his alcoholic qualifications, and he has left us the earliest description of the Military Road, from Cruagh to Laragh, while he reports Glencree Barracks as already 'useless' (fortification was still part of a gentleman's education, hence Trotter's interest).

Earlier marches through the mountains were almost all strictly military, and those who like historical puzzles can work out the route followed by Richard II, or by Strongbow's army, en route to attack Dublin. Liam Price has published his theory of the Anglo-Norman line of march (in the *An Oige Review*, Vol. I, No. 11), and this route is supported by old records and by surviving tradition – at least in Allagour, Glenasmole, where a farmer once told me that the track I had just descended, north-east down the flank of Seahan, was used 'by thousands of men, long ago'.

Before the beginnings of An Oige or of the Irish Mountaineering Club, epic walks were done in Wicklow, and not least by locals. In Kilmacanogue they still talk of Tom Hill of Kilmurray, who won a race to the top of Great Sugar Loaf and back, from Kilmacanogue

Graveyard gate, in some seconds over twenty-nine minutes. Then there was Furlong of Rathdangan, who ran from Rathdangan to Rathdrum, and who refused a lift from a cart he overtook in Greenan, remarking 'I'm in a hurry!'; to say nothing of Brennan, the Dublin baker, who every Friday evening set off to walk through the night to Tinahely, arriving there at 7 a.m.

Across the Victorian scene strides the almost legendary figure of H.C. Hart, whose gruelling journey across the high tops, from Terenure to Lugnacullia and back, remained uneclipsed until 1927, though surpassed upon several subsequent occasions. Hart's high-level route has become the 'Lug Walk', organised in recent years by the Irish Ramblers Club every second year.

Less well known are Pentland and Craig, two worthies of Trinity, who, about 1875, marched from Botany Bay to the Chair of Croghan and back in 'a day and two nights, without stopping', by a route of which we know only that it included Tonelagee summit.

So much for bygone marathons, although it is worth recording that twenty years before An Oige opened their first hostel beside Lough Dan, the idea of a walkers' club-hut, permanently located in the mountains, was proposed by Standish O'Grady, in the columns of *The Irish Times* but the suggestion apparently shocked those Edwardians into silence, for the hitherto lively correspondence immediately lapsed (it had begun as a discussion of the best way to climb Lugnacullia).

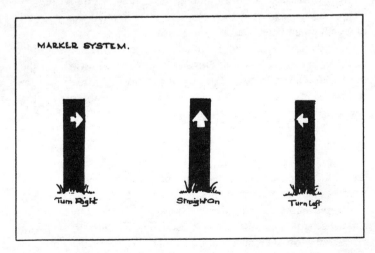

Car Parks on the Wicklow Way

Location	Route Sketch	Remarks
Marlay North Gate	1	large closes at
Marlay South Gate	1	large varying hours
Kilmashogue Forest Entrance	3	large
Curtlestown Forest Entrance	11	4 cars only
Knockree Forest Entrance	12	2 cars only
Lackan Wood Entrance	12	fairly large
Crone Forest Entrance	12	large
Luggala Forest Entrance	17	large
Luggala Road	—	10 cars only
Pier Gates Layby	18	large
Sleamaine Forest Entrance	18	4 cars only
Oldbridge, Lough Dan Road	21	large
Laragh Forest (Glenmacnass)	24	2 cars only
Brockagh Forest Entrance	25	4 cars only
Laragh Village	26	large
Glendalough, Visitors' Centre	28	large; free; closes at varying times
Glendalough, Lower Car Park	—	large; free
Glendalough, Upper Lake	—	large; fees
Glenmalure, Logrania	—	1km from Way
Coolalingo Bridge	37	4 cars only
Drumgoff Crossroads opposite Glenmalure Lodge	37	large
Drumgoff Gap	41	4 cars only
Carrickashane Forest Entrance	42	2 cars only
Forest Entrance, Brown Mt. Road	44	2 cars only
Forest Entrance, Brown Mt. Road	45	2 cars only
Iron Bridge, Picnic Site	46	10 cars only
Ballyteigue Bridge	47	2 cars only
Sheilstown Forest Entrance	51	2 cars only
Moyne Boreen, N end	55	1 car only
Moyne Boreen, S end	55	1 car only
Ballycumber Forest, N Entrance	55	2 cars only
Ballycumber Forest, S Entrance	56	2 cars only
Wooden Bridge	61	2 cars only
Muskeagh Forest Entrance	63	2 cars only
Mullinacuff Post Office	64	2 cars only
Raheenakit Forest, N Entrance	68	2 cars only
Raheenakit Forest, S Entrance	68	2 cars only
Moylisha Forest Entrance	72	2 cars only
Newry Forest Entrance	73	2 cars only
Clonegal Village	75	large

Wicklow Way Distance Table (kms)

DAY ONE *The First Walk*

Location	Sketch No.	Intermediate distances	Distances from Marlay Park	Distances from Clonegal
Marlay Park N. Gate	(1)	....	....	131.1
		2.8		
Kilmashogue Forest Entrance	(3)	....	2.8	128.3
		6.5		
Glencullen Road	(7)	....	9.3	121.8
		2.3		
Boranaraltry Bridge	(8)	....	11.6	119.5
		3.4		
Dublin/Wicklow Boundary	(11)	....	15.0	116.1
		2.5		
Curtlestown Forest Entrance	(11)	....	17.5	113.6
		1.0		
Lackan Wood Entrance	(12)	....	18.5	112.6
Knockree Hostel		....		
		3.3		

DAY TWO *The Second Walk*

Location	Sketch No.	Intermediate distances	Distances from Marlay Park	Distances from Clonegal
Glencree River Footbridge	(13)	....	21.8	109.3
		0.6		
Crone Car Park	(13)	....	22.4	108.7
		2.5		
Ride Rock Summit	(14)	....	24.9	106.2
		1.3		
Dargle Footbridge	(15)	....	26.2	104.9
		0.8		
Deerpark Forest edge	(15)	....	27.0	104.1
		2.6		
White Hill Saddle	(16)	....	29.6	101.5
		0.6		

Location	Sketch No.	Intermediate distances	Distances from Marlay Park	Distances from Clonegal
White Hill Summit	(17)	....	30.2	100.9
		1.1		
The Barr Summit	(17)	....	31.3	99.8
		1.2		
Luggala Forest Car Park	(17)	....	32.5	98.6
		1.2		
Sleamaine Forest Entrance	(18)	....	33.7	97.4
		4.8		
Roundwood Road Junction	(21)	....	38.5	92.6
		1.3		

DAY THREE *The Third Walk*

Location	Sketch No.	Intermediate distances	Distances from Marlay Park	Distances from Clonegal
Oldbridge Junction	(21)	....	39.8	91.3
		4.7		
Paddock Hill Path	(23)	....	44.5	86.6
		1.6		
Glenmacnass (Military Road)	(24)	....	46.1	85.0
		1.0		
Brockagh Forest Entrance	(25)	....	47.1	84.0
		1.1		

(Glendalough Hostel 2km W)

DAY FOUR *The Fourth Walk*

Location	Sketch No.	Intermediate distances	Distances from Marlay Park	Distances from Clonegal
Junction for Green Road	(27)	....	48.2	82.9
		4.0		
Information Centre	(29)	....	52.2	78.9
		0.3		
Junction with Forest Road	(30)	....	52.5	78.6
		0.9		
Junction below Derrybawn	(31)	....	53.4	77.7
		4.5		

Location	Sketch No.	Intermediate distances	Distances from Marlay Park	Distances from Clonegal
Borenacrow	(33)	.... 2.7	57.9	73.2
Junction for Glenmalure Hostel	(35)	.... 3.6	60.6	70.5
Drumgoff Crossroads	(37)	.... 5.0	64.2	66.9
Start of Forest Road Slieve Maan	(40)	.... 3.3	69.2	61.9
Drumgoff Gap	(41)	.... 2.1	72.5	58.6
Forest Road Carrickashane	(42)	.... 1.7	74.6	56.5
Brown Mountain Road	(44)	.... 1.3	76.3	54.8
Iron Bridge, Ow River	(46)	.... 2.0	77.6	53.4

DAY FIVE *The Fifth Walk*

Location	Sketch No.	Intermediate distances	Distances from Marlay Park	Distances from Clonegal
Ballyteigue Bridge	(47)	.... 4.1	79.6	51.5
Shielstown Forest Entrance	(51)	.... 2.7	83.7	47.4
Moyne Village (junction for)	(53)	.... 3.7	86.4	44.7
Ballycumber (Old Schoolhouse)	(56)	.... 3.4	90.1	41.0
Monument Cross	(58)	.... 4.7	93.5	37.6
Tinahely Road	(61)	.... 4.4	98.2	32.9

DAY SIX *The Sixth Walk*

Location	Sketch No.	Intermediate distances	Distances from Marlay Park	Distances from Clonegal
Muskeagh Forest	(63)	....	102.6	28.5
		1.2		
Junction in Mullinacuff	(64)	....	103.8	27.3
		1.7		
Stranakelly Crossroads	(65)	....	105.5	25.6
		3.0		
Kilquiggan Catholic Church	(66)	....	108.5	22.6
		2.1		
T-junction, Boley	(67)	....	110.6	20.5
		1.2		
Junction for Raheenakit	(67)	....	111.8	19.3
		2.1		

DAY SEVEN *The Seventh Walk*

Location	Sketch No.	Intermediate distances	Distances from Marlay Park	Distances from Clonegal
Raheenakit Forest Gate Entrance	(68)	....	113.9	17.2
		4.0		
Junction, Aghowle Lower	(71)	....	117.9	13.2
		0.6		
Junction for Mill of Purgatory	(71)	....	118.5	12.6
		1.6		
T-junction for Money Upper	(71)	....	120.1	11.0
		1.0		
Moylisha Forest Entrance	(72)	....	121.1	10.0
		5.4		
Urelands Forest Entrance	(73)	....	126.5	4.6
		1.7		
T-junction Wicklow Bridge	(75)	....	128.2	2.9
		1.1		
Junction for Sandhill House	(75)	....	129.3	1.8
		1.8		
Clonegal	(75)	....	131.1	....

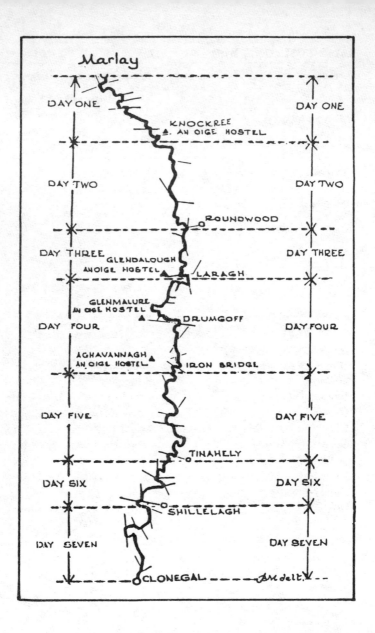

Day One . The First Walk

Marlay Park to Knockree An Oige Hostel

Distance: 22km   *Time:* 6-7 hours

Route Outline   Marlay Park – Whitechurch Bridge – Kilmashogue Lane – Kilmashogue Forest Road – Tibradden Forest Firebreak – Glencullen Road – Boranaraltry Bridge – Glencullen Forest Road – Path to Curtlestown Forest – Forest Road – North Road, Glencree – Knockree Boreen – Forest Road – Knockree Boreen – Knockree Hostel.

Parking   Marlay Park – Kilmashogue Forest Entrance – Curtlestown Forest Entrance – Knockree Forest Entrance – Lackan Wood Entrance – Knockree Hostel.

Marlay Park lies outside Rathfarnham and is a public park with sports facilities, craft centre, coffee shop and pleasant grounds. It contains two large parking areas – but the gates close at different times depending on the season. The park closes at 5 p.m. in winter (November-January) and at 9 p.m. in summer (May-August). Closing time varies for the other months as follows: 8 p.m. April, September; 7 p.m. October; 6 p.m. February, March. Obviously hours of daylight are the guiding principle in what would otherwise be an eccentric arrangement. It would not be fun, after a day's walking, to find your car locked in the park for the night or to find irate attendants awaiting your arrival! The opening time, 10 a.m., remains the same throughout the year.

Marlay Park may also be reached by bus – take Dublin Bus no. 47B from Hawkins Street (in the city centre) to the north gate.

On the route out from Rathfarnham there are three gates into the park. Look out for the signpost indicating Marlay Craft Centre. This is the north gate, with a large car park immediately inside, near the house.

The Wicklow Way starts here with Marlay House itself on your right. You set off south on the tarmac path towards the playing fields, past the broad lawns, fine trees and ornamental lakes. There

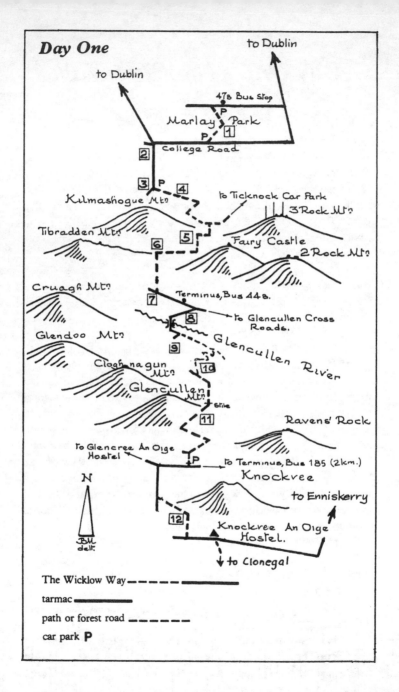

Day One

to Dublin

to Dublin

47B Bus Stop
P
Marlay Park
P 1
2 College Road
3 P 4
Kilmashogue Mtn.
to Ticknock Car Park
3 Rock Mtn.
Tibradden Mtn.
5
6 Fairy Castle
2 Rock Mtn.
Cruagh Mtn.
7 Terminus, Bus 44B.
8 to Glencullen Cross Roads.
Glendoo Mtn.
9 Glencullen River
Clogh na gun Mtn.
10
Glencullen Mtn.
Stile
11 Ravens' Rock
To Glencree An Oige Hostel
P to Terminus, Bus 185 (2km.)
Knockree
N
to Enniskerry
12 Knockree An Oige Hostel.
B.M. dell.
to Clonegal

The Wicklow Way – – – – –
tarmac ▬▬▬▬
path or forest road – – – – – –
car park **P**

32

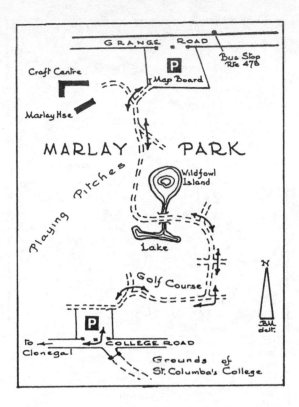

is as yet hardly a hint of the mountain barriers ahead until you reach the first marker beyond the football pitches. Here you can see the ridge of the Fairy Castle Mountain and catch a glimpse of the Three Rock Mountain, which is unmistakable with its array of radio link masts.

Plans for the south ring highway will, some time in the future, sweep away most of this strip of the park.

Continuing in this direction you will eventually reach the south gate of Marlay, emerging onto College Road, near St Columba's College (Sketch 1). Turn right on leaving this gate to head west on College Road (as this is a busy road, walk single file on the right, facing oncoming traffic). There is a slight downhill before you bear left to cross Whitechurch Bridge (O 148 255) and then turn left up Kilmashogue Lane (Sketch 2). Like most Co. Dublin roads, this lane has been supplied with rather suburban-looking name plates,

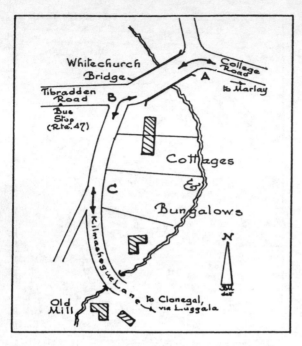

Sketch 2

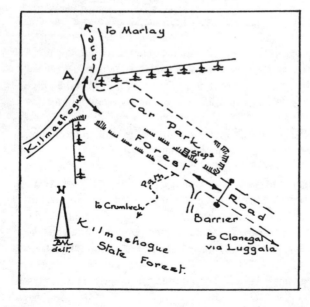

Sketch 3

Sketch 4

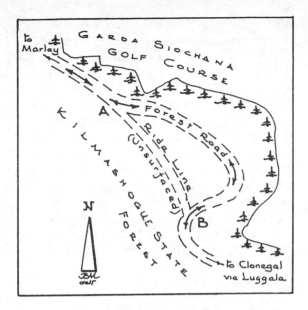

but it still has a mountain-type flavour, rising more and more steeply as you head south, with a final twist on a one-in-seven grade before you turn left into Kilmashogue Wood car park (A, Sketch 3).

Dublin city spreads below this car park, but the Hell Fire Club ruin crowning Mountpelier Hill, is the only summit in sight, to westward away on your left. Stories abound of the shenanigans reputed to have gone on here where the Rake-Helly Club is said to have met in the eighteenth century. This was a club for high-society gentlemen which met in Dublin city. They indulged in black magic, toasts to the devil and tests of endurance which involved burning the meeting room with the members inside – the last man out had proved he could survive hell's fire longest and was the winner. Whether or not these activities went on on the mountain top is not known. A hunting lodge was built there in 1760 by one Squire Conolly, on the summit. In the course of construction an ancient stone circle was partially demolished, and later during a violent storm the roof was struck by lightning – superstition blamed the interference with the ancient remains. It is possible that stories of the devil and the Rake-Helly Club became enmeshed forever with this event.

Later, the lodge was re-roofed in stone, and during Queen

Victoria's visit a splendid bonfire was built and burned on this roof – it survived this onslaught and is still there.

A few steps go up from the parking area to the level of the forest road, and before you now is the first of about a dozen steel-bar barriers that lie between you and the trail's end in Clonegal.

These barriers have been used by the Forestry Commission since about 1975. They are said to be more durable than wooden gates, but they are hardly an obstacle to motor-cyclists.

As you head east along this forest road, you will hear and see glimpses of the golfers on the nearby Garda Siochána course, but for wide views you have to wait till two sharp bends and rises have been put behind you. When the road levels off, the view ahead shows the array of radio-link and other masts on the upper slopes of Three Rock Mountain. This is really a lower shoulder of Two Rock Mountain, whose western ridge you have now to cross to get to Glencullen.

The route of the Way here has had to be changed three times, firstly to avoid traffic on Ticknock Forest road (servicing the

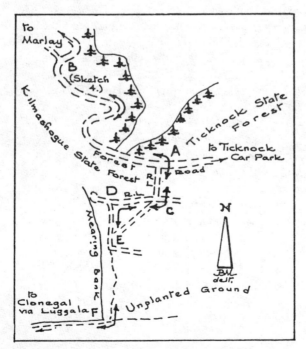

Sketch 5

Sketch 6

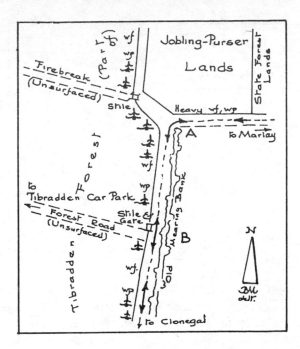

various masts), secondly to fit in with forest changes, and thirdly to keep away from the badly eroded area in the soft black turf west of Fairy Castle (545m), the highest point of the Two Rock and Three Rock group.

Sketches 5 and 6 show how you get up to the crest of the broad ridge linking Fairy Castle to Tibradden Mountain (467m), using ride lines, then a path south through some unplanted forest ground. The Way thus reaches the ridge crest (F, Sketch 5), partly avoiding an eroded stretch WSW of the Fairy Castle summit. Standing now at about 460m, you look south to see all Glencullen, backed by another, slightly higher ridge, stretching from Ravens' Rock (SE), by Glencullen Mountain and Cloghnagun, to where Glendoo and Cruagh Mountains merge into the Featherbed, itself only a shoulder of Cruagh, just south of west.

The Way goes around rather than over this next ridge, and the key to the crossing is in that long stripe of forest planted under Glencullen Mountain. But first you have to drop down to the Glencullen road, beginning with a turn right to head west along the ridge to a sort of T-junction (A, Sketch 6, O 157 219). Here a left turn

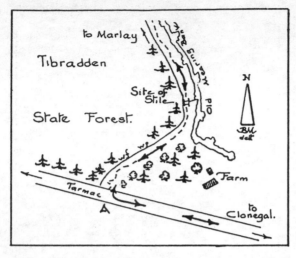

Sketch 7

puts you on a rough firebreak between the forest fence and an old mearing bank, dividing the open mountain from tillage lands. The firebreak has had drainage channels dug across it at frequent intervals, which make for tiring walking.

The firebreak drops steeply to where a stile once stood (Sketch 7), from which a path leads down to the Glencullen road. Turning left, the tarmac road is followed for 1.5km to the hairpin turn right, down to Boranaraltry Bridge, a stone structure rebuilt after the great 1905 flood, and so well rebuilt that in a flood exactly eighty-one years later to the day, the bridge was unharmed, though parts of Bray were again devastated.

South of the bridge continue straight, ignoring the steep boreen (B, Sketch 8) on the right, to climb gradually to a gate with dire warnings about parking and blocking access. Beyond the gate the road becomes a forest road and at a second gate you pass through a kissing gate and continue to a junction, where you go right to zigzag up through the recently-planted area. On the zigzags up through the woods you change from one map to the next, walking off Sheet 50 and onto Sheet 56. As you climb wide views open up back north over the ground already travelled, down over the field patterns of Glencullen, a glen which, despite its nearness to Dublin and despite many new buildings, still retains a certain lonely mountain air.

The forest road then straightens out as you head SE, still

Sketch 8

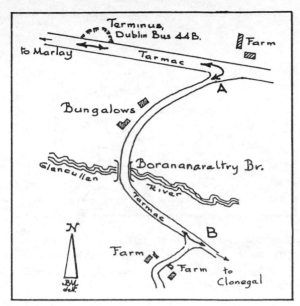

Sketch 9

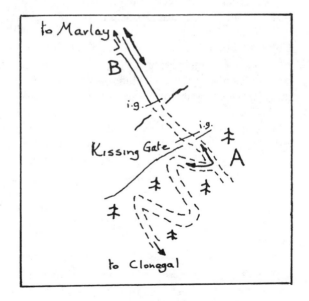

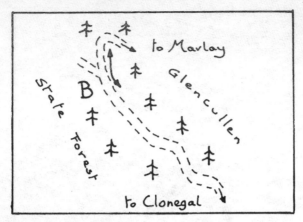

climbing, and is joined by another road from the right (B, Sketch 10) where you continue straight to reach a turntable at the forest boundary, which is also the boundary of counties Dublin and Wicklow (Sketch 11).

Here the official route slants off east to join a firebreak on the edge of a forest extension ahead. However, this official line, over broken ground with deep heather, was treated with chemicals to make a path and the result has been a quagmire of squelchy black turf. Remedial work has been carried out by Conservation Volunteers Ireland, but if you find it in this condition an alternative route may be taken by turning right when you come out by the gap from Glencullen Forest, climbing to the forest corner and taking the parallel path to the firebreak on the end of the forest extension.

The firebreak often has great pools between its slabby rocks, but there is no real difficulty except after severe winter frost, when I once found the going here tough enough, with ice crusting every pool, and the rocks themselves coated with verglas (or ice-glaze).

This firebreak path leads straight to a stile and gap in the fence of Curtlestown Forest, with only the thick post of an old timber signpost on the left (B, Sketch 11).

Beyond the fence you enter one of the most magical sections of the Way.

The path goes down through rocks. The trees here (at 450m) are scattered as if self-sown, and do not block the views towards the deeps of Glencree. Across the glen, impressive Maulin, majestic Djouce and bulky Tonduff Mountains fill the sky. This is a good

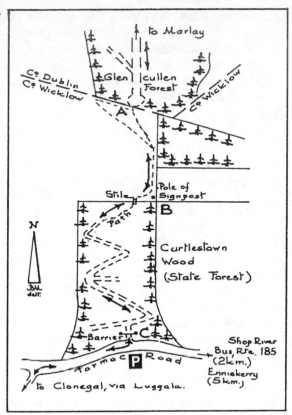

place to sit and relax, to gaze eastward towards Bray Head, with Great and Little Sugar Loaf Mountains showing the contrast between the Cambrian rocks and the mica schist, while to westward rise the bulky granite domes of Central Wicklow.

The 'arrowy peak' of Great Sugar Loaf (501m), is pretty near a perfect cone from this angle, making it the most distinctive summit on the whole Wicklow Way. The name, of course, comes from the cone-shaped 'loaf' in which sugar was sold, till, after 1800, granulated and lump sugar became common.

Just because of its prominent form, Great Sugar Loaf has attracted all kinds of attention down the years. When Charles Stewart Parnell, leader of the Irish Parliamentary Party and Home Rule advocate, died in 1891, a scheme was worked out to build a sort of lighthouse on the summit – to be fitted with giant mirrors reflecting the sun over the whole area! Money was actually subscribed for this outlandish scheme, but was in fact used some sixty years later for the benefit of the children's library in Bray.

The path continues under close-planted trees, a few rocks breaking the brown carpet of dead pine needles. As it goes down southerly, the path becomes a ride line, then it joins a forest road on which you zigzag down to the forest entrance barrier (C, Sketch 11).

The Way turns right on to a tarmac road here, and this road is followed for the next 250m – so walk carefully keeping an eye out for traffic, which can be heavy at weekends on the section from Curtlestown Forest entrance to the turn (left) on to the Knockree boreen (A, Sketch 12). This boreen gives wide views west, up Glencree to Kippure Mountain with its TV mast and its twin cliff-bound hollows sheltering Upper and Lower Lough Bray (the lower is the larger and has an underwater cliff, similar to those of Loch Ness, so not surprisingly a large unknown creature has been reported swimming there!).

The TV building on Kippure top is dwarfed by the tall mast with its array of stays and guy ropes. This mast was brought up in sections, and assembled by Norwegian specialists, who said that they had rigged similar masts all over Europe but nowhere had they met such weather as they did on Kippure. On a typical day, it would be dead calm at 9 a.m. and freezing hard, with icicles six foot long, hanging from the stay wires. By 10 a.m. a thaw set in, no outside work was possible and everyone took shelter in the station building as the outsize icicles came crashing down, one damaging the station roof. At noon, a full gale brought lashing rain, but by 4 p.m. frost gripped Kippure again, covering the access road with glassy black ice while cars and trucks in the open were sheeted in ice themselves.

The same access road to Kippure TV station revived a construction method used in prehistoric Ireland, to cross the deep bog SE of Kippure summit. A 'corduroy' road was built, using bundles of fifteen-foot poles, about thirty thousand poles in all, making a timber raft on which the road itself was laid, just as our ancient ancestors did in various midland bogs.

The Wicklow Way turns left on a forest road into Lackan Wood, (C, Sketch 12), which was first planted by the Powerscourt Estate, but has been state forest for many years now. Felling has been

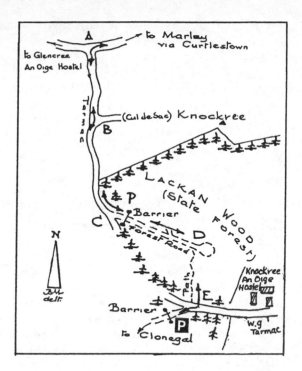

going on since about 1985, so it is anybody's guess whether the fine old Scots pines on the SW edge of the wood will survive – but trees are a crop like any other, to be harvested when ripe. J.M. Synge often walked in Glencree, and timber-working here inspired the lines

> Men as trees walking
> And all to be cut down.

With this sobering thought, turn down south through the young trees to reach a tarmac road (E, Sketch 12), where Knockree An Oige Hostel is barely five minutes away to the left, offering companionship, comfort and shelter after your first day on the Way.

VARIATIONS

Variation One: Tibradden Summit

Distance: 2km (extra)   *Time*: 1 hour (extra)

Tibradden summit (O 148 222) rises about 1km NW of the Way. It is reached by a rough forest track, starting from B, Sketch 6. There is a prehistoric burial at the highest point (467m), and some scribings of doubtful date on the north-facing rock-slab SE of the cairn. The return to the Way is by the same route.

Variation Two: Glencullen Mountain

Distance: 1.5km; same as direct route   *Time:* 1 hour; same as direct route

Prince William's Seat (O 177 183) is half a kilometre from the trail, and on a clear day is a great viewpoint. From the turntable end of the Glencullen Forest road (Sketch 11) turn right, up by the forest edge, then on SW by the county boundary, to the top at 556m, with a survey pillar and damaged cairn. Both Glencullen and Glencree spread below, and I have more than once seen the Welsh mountains eastward.

To rejoin the Way, head down SSE to reach a firebreak at the edge of younger trees. Turn left to contour east above Curtlestown Forest. At a T-junction in firebreaks turn left again and about 100m takes you to the stile and gap in the fence (B, Sketch 11) from where you follow the Way once more.

Shorter Walks – Day One Area

(Marlay-Knockree)

Motorists parking at Marlay Park do not have a wide choice of shorter, circular walks near the start of the Wicklow Way, but obviously if a car pick-up can be arranged, the choice is widened.

1. *The First Fringes: Marlay – Ticknock – Marlay*

Distance: 11.5km   *Time*: 4 to 4½ hours

Route Outline   Marlay North Gate (car park) – South Gate – College Road – Kilmashogue Forest Entrance – Forest Road – Ticknock Forest Road – Ticknock Forest Car Park – Kellystown Road – College Road – Marlay South Gate – North Gate Car Park.

The Wicklow Way is followed only as far as junction A, Sketch 5. Keep straight ahead here, to a forest barrier and T-junction where you go left, having level and downhill walking from this on.

The varied array of radio masts on the crest of Three Rock Mountain is only about 500m away from the barrier just mentioned, so your forest road doubles as an access road for the trucks and vans servicing the masts, besides forest traffic (on weekdays). From here on keep well in to the right, walking single file, facing oncoming traffic, although the trees now thin out on your left, opening fine wide views westwards across the forests you have traversed, showing the bare unplanted dome of Kilmashogue Mountain (408m) (O 158 237), the nearest summit to the centre of Dublin.

Behind, and to the left of Kilmashogue, is the Hell Fire Club, atop Mountpelier Hill, with a steep-sided cleft cutting it off from the main mountains. This cleft is Piperstown Glen (O 115 233), a remarkable relic of Ice Age times. Geologists say it is a spillway cut by great torrents of melt water, released when a giant glacier that once filled Glenasmole began to thaw.

This westward view is cut down as you drop towards the next landmark, also on the left, but right beside your road. This is a series of very much gapped earthen banks, partly faced in concrete, mostly grass-grown now, all once part of Ticknock rifle range.

Set up by the British War Office about 1900, Ticknock came into its own in the 1940-45 period, when the severe petrol shortage forced the powers that be to train the Dublin garrison as close as possible to their base.

Next you come to smaller, then taller trees, to where the forest road twists and bends, reaching the forest barrier and the car park, which, at weekends, is one of the busiest, being so near the south Dublin suburbs. Turn right onto the tarmac road then quickly left at the large rocks, descending to join tarmac again. Turn right when you join the Ticknock road (O 168 242), still going downhill, with most of the city of Dublin spread below and ahead of you.

But you must also watch the traffic, and look out for a turn left (O 169 244) – this puts you onto the Kellystown road, still descending, twisting and bending. You pass a prominent knob of granite on the right, partly quarried away. How many tons of granite window sills, how many lordly flights of entrance steps to Victorian mansions came out of that Stackstown quarry? How many generations of under-housemaids brushed down those same steps before the Victorian age was 'changed, changed utterly'? This is a question hardly solvable on the last leg of your walk, as you come to the Grange Lodge Pub and B & B (on the right) and then to a crossroads (O 160 257) where you go left, onto College Road once more, back again to the South Gate of Marlay Park, turning in right there to retrace the route across Marlay, to your waiting car at the North Gate car park.

Motorists who can organise a second driver to go around to Ticknock Forest car park to wait for them, can start at Kimashogue Forest car park (A, Sketch 3), finishing at Ticknock. This reduces the walk to just 5km, and the time to 3 hours.

Walkers using buses, by starting from the Dublin Bus No. 47 stop near Whitechurch Bridge, (Sketch 2), reduce the walk to 9km, and the time to 3 hours also, while the same time and distance (11.5km, 4 hours) is involved for walkers who, instead of going back through Marlay using Kellystown Road, keep straight ahead at Ticknock crossroads, (O 168 255), to pick up the Ballinteer bus (No. 48A) on the Dublin side of a junction (O 171 268).

2. *Marlay – Glencullen Bus Terminus* (No. 44B)

Distance: 13km   *Time*: 4-5 hours

Follow the Wicklow Way from Marlay Park to the bus lay-by in Glencullen, see Sketches 1 to 8, inclusive. As the No. 44B is an infrequent service, check times in the current Dublin Bus timetable. The only tarmac road in Glencullen is narrow, and has no lay-bys above Johnnie Fox's pub at Glencullen crossroads (O 189 204), so this and the shorter route 3, below, do not suit motorists.

3. *Glencullen Bus Terminus* (No. 44B) – *Curtlestown Forest Entrance* – *Shop River Bus Terminus* (No. 185)

Distance: 9.33km   *Time*: 3-4 hours

Follow the Way to Curtlestown Forest Entrance (Sketches 8 to 11 inclusive), turn left there, walking on tarmac for the next 2.5km, on a road which becomes decidedly busy at weekends. Curtlestown Catholic church (a small gothic-style building) is passed on your left, with farmhouses nearby – a small place indeed (O 192 166), its name corrupted from 'Thorkill's town', the home of some otherwise unknown Norse settler. You pass a turn right (signposted for Knockree An Oige Hostel), then the Shop River bus terminus is only half a kilometre ahead (O 203 171).

The name Shop River is now firmly entrenched in the bus timetables, but I have never heard a local person use it, and neither a shop nor a river is to be seen there. The No. 185 bus goes steeply down into Enniskerry, where you can transfer to the more frequent No. 44, or else sit tight and go on to Bray station, to link with the streamlined DART rail service (Dublin Area Rapid Transit) which heads for the city centre, and on around the north shore of Dublin Bay, right on to Howth.

4. *Curtlestown Forest*

Distance: 4km   *Time*: 1-1½ hours

Route Outline   Curtlestown Forest Entrance – Forest Road Zigzags – Grassy Path – Forest Road – Forest Entrance.

This short trip suits motorists, who use the car park at C, Sketch 11. Start by following the Way up the forest road, which climbs in zigzags, after you leave the area of younger trees (Sketch 11). Higher up, the trees frame views back across Glencree to the impressive form of Maulin, unmistakable with that sort of step breaking the outline of the shoulder to the right of the top, and to its bigger, bulkier neighbour Tonduff Mountain (the name meaning 'black backside'). When the forest road slants up towards the edge of the trees (the edge on the left, as you face uphill) you come to another wide bend, where, on the left, an enticing path goes down, between the trees and the forest fence. This is your way back to the car at the forest gate, back down the grassy path, which twists slightly to avoid a few self-sown trees, then settles to a steady gradual descent.

This is a great place to introduce children to hill walking, to let them play the 'Indian game' – getting them to move utterly silently for five minutes or so, as if in hostile territory, and of course the winner is the one who hears the greatest number of sounds: the strange creak of tree branch on tree branch, the harsh croak of a raven, even the muted roar of the cascades called O'Toole's Buttermilk, far across Glencree (O 176 137); but for this last sound, you need a strong south-westerly wind.

The path joins the end of a forest road, on which you go left, for less than half a kilometre, then, lo and behold – you are back at the original T-junction and down on your right, barely five minutes away, is the forest entrance barrier and your car.

Day Two . The Second Walk

Knockree to Roundwood

Distance: 20km   *Time*: 6-7 hours

Route Outline   Knockree Hostel – Footbridge – Maulin Wood – Ride Rock – Dargle Ford – Djouce Shoulder Track – White Hill – The Barr – Luggala Car Park – Sleamaine Forest Road – Lake Park Crossroads – Roundwood.

Parking   Knockree Hostel – Lake Car Park (2km SE of Way) – R759 about 0.5km NW of Luggula Forest Entrance – Luggala Forest Entrance – Luggala Road – Pier Gates Layby – Sleamaine Forest Entrance – Roundwood.

If you have not stayed overnight at Knockree Hostel but have used Enniskerry, Bray or Dublin – or of course if you are not doing the Way in one continuous walk – you may drive to the parking place at E, Sketch 12, 0.5km west of Knockree Hostel. Alternatively, you could take the No. 185 bus (Bray – Enniskerry – Shop River). Taking the bus adds about 3km to the day's journey – starting from the bus stop head west on the road, forking left at the hostel signpost. Turn down to the right at a hairpin bend near the old Annacrivey Schoolhouse (O 199 160) to rejoin the Way at E, Sketch 12.

From the forest barrier (O 189 150), follow the forest road past another joining from the left. Watch out for a marker directing you left on a small path to a fence. Crossing the stile, follow the fence down to the river bank and turn left to continue on the footbridge. Once across the river follow the path, keeping the river on your right, to join a forest road leading uphill to the tarmac road on the southern side of Glencree. Turn left here for Crone Forest car park (O 193 142). Go right through the parking area. Passing the barrier, continue to the junction and a map board. The Way then twists uphill (B, Sketch 13), crosses a bridge over a stream (usually dry), then runs dead straight for a kilometre, pretty well boxed in by trees.

This has been called a monotonous section, but the good wine is

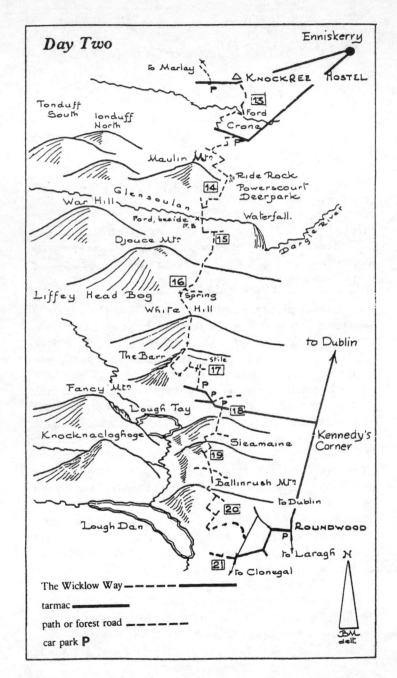

Day Two

Enniskerry

to Marley
P
△ KNOCKREE HOSTEL
13
Ford
Crone
P

Tonduff South
Tonduff North
Maulin Mtn
to Ride Rock
Powerscourt Deerpark
14

Glensoulan
War Hill
Ford, beside F.B
Waterfall.
15
Dargle River

Djouce Mtn
16
Spring
Liffey Head Bog
White Hill

The Barr
stile
17
to Dublin

Fancy Mtn
P
P
P
18
Lough Tay

Knocknacloghoge
Sieamaine
19
Kennedy's Corner

Ballinrush Mtn?
to Dublin
20

Lough Dan
P
ROUNDWOOD
to Laragh N
21
to Clonegal

The Wicklow Way ------
tarmac ━━━
path or forest road ------
car park P

BM delt.

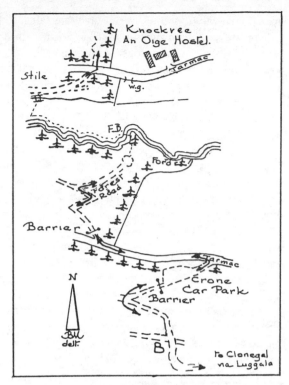

still in reserve. The first sign of change is when birch and old beeches line the track. Next, the road widens to something like an outsize turntable, and another forest road slants off left (A, Sketch 14). The Way climbs in one zigzag to about 300m, then rises straight and steadily beyond the planted ground, where you realise that a tremendous view is about to spread before you. The track dwindles to a path, curves south around the small outcrop called Ride Rock, and the whole Powerscourt Deerpark lies below, backed by the Great Sugar Loaf peak almost due east and by Djouce Mountain, about SSW.

The patterns of planting in the Deerpark, seen from Ride Rock, tell a great deal about the history of the glen. The wall of conifers climbing the eastern slope is obviously state forestry, laced with roads planned for timber extraction, while the flat glen floor, where the Dargle River curves and winds, has far earlier planting, scattered oaks, a few pines, and a road to bring tourists to the picnic green at the very foot of Powerscourt Waterfall.

You are gazing down upon eighteenth-century landscape planning by the Powerscourt (now Slazenger) Estate, but after two world wars the Deerpark was so bereft of trees that the state moved in to plant all but the narrow stripe now shown without trees on the O.S. Sheet 56 map (O 203 125).

Take the Ride Rock path (Sketch 14) (another legacy of Powerscourt planning) which runs almost level for the next kilometre, giving endless variations of the great Ride Rock view. The Way passes under a high jagged wall of mica schist rock. Look out now for a path going diagonally right up into very close-planted trees. Take this rising path which soon levels off, then trends left, downhill, to sunshine again and to a sort of T-junction with another path (A, Sketch 15).

A right turn here on this well-trodden path leads to a totally vandalised stile, now only a gap in the forest fence. Here the route goes left, downhill to the Dargle River, down the space between the original Deerpark stone wall and the forest fence.

This reaches the Dargle at what was once the Watergates, where a large gate once filled the gap across the river in the wall to keep the deer in the park. This has long since vanished and a footbridge subsequently erected was demolished in the great August storm of

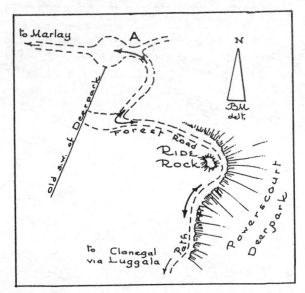

Sketch 14

Sketch 15

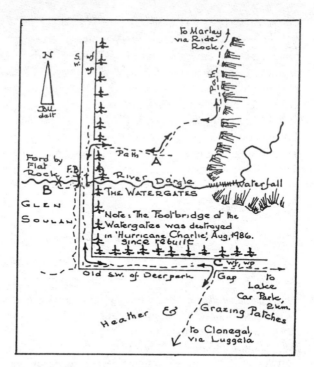

1986. However, a bridge has since been erected and is now the responsibility of the National Parks and Wildlife Service, as most of the area here has been acquired by that body and forms part of the Wicklow National Park.

An old crossing still survives also, an easy ford by flat rocks, only a few moments upstream of the Watergates.

South of the ford, a path climbs south, alongside the Deerpark wall. There is another path inside the wall, useful on windy days, but half-choked with fern in late summer.

Either way, halt at the corner of the stone wall, where it and the forest fence turn east, and look back over Glensoulan Valley, north towards Maulin and Tonduff Mountains, with the Ride Rock shoulder prominent to the NE. Glensoulan has been empty of people since before 1800; it was once famous for crops of rye and some traces of old tillage and house sites can still be made out westwards as you come up south from the Dargle ford. Keep on by the wall, about SE, for some 240m, until the ground levels out and you see a gap in the wall on the right (C, Sketch 15); this marks the

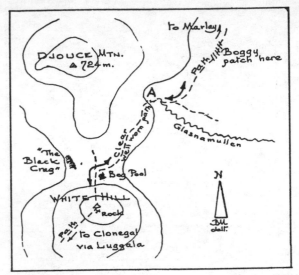

start of the section across the 'heather deserts', the bare heart of Wicklow, shelterless and almost unchanged since Mr Neville, in 1760, wrote across his detailed map of Wicklow: 'This vast tract of mountain and bog is uninhabited'.

This is still true today and, just beyond the river, the notion took you to walk westwards along grid line 112 on the O.S. map till you met an inhabited house, you would have to trek for 18km across very rough country. For the first 13km you would not even *see* a house.

So this is the place to gird your loins, so to speak, checking rucksack straps for comfort, making sure that map and compass are handy. Then you start a gradual rise for 2km on a well-used path, to surmount the eastern shoulder of Djouce Mountain, at about 530m, with ever-widening views east. A descent follows to the source of the Glasnamullen, a spring of good water (A, Sketch 16), followed by a much steeper climb to the saddle between Djouce and White Hill.

When the trail crests the rise, there is a view westward over central Wicklow almost as fine as that from Djouce summit – a tumbled mass of mountains, ridge on ridge, while back eastwards all the fields of Calary plains, the twin Vartry reservoirs, perhaps even Wales on really clear days, reward your efforts.

The Way turns left to go south now, by a wide, boggy path over

Sketch 17

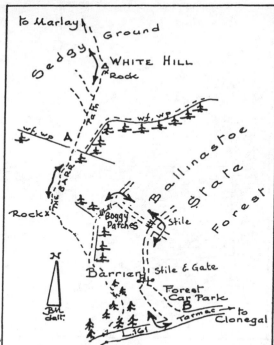

to Marlay

Sedgy Ground

WHITE HILL
Rock

Path

wf, wp

wf, wp A

Rock×

THE BARR

Boggy Patches

Stile

Ballinastoe State Forest

N

BM. dell:

Barrier

Stile & Gate

Forest Car Park

B

Tarmac

to Clonegal

L.161

Sketch 18

to Marlay

Ballinastoe State Forest

The Pier Gates

The Murdering Steps

wf, wp

Lay By

P

L.161 Tarmac

Archer's Road (private)

A

old Keelin's

to Round Wood

Barrier

P

N

BM. dell:

Sleamaine Road

Forest

Forest Road

to Clonegal via Laragh

55

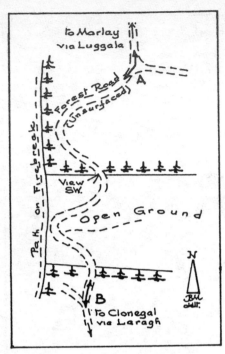

the sedgy dome of White Hill (no cairn, 630m). As the descent starts, your path trends SW, down to a gap in the fence (A, Sketch 17) and straight on along a ridge called the Barr. (A memorial to the author of this book, J.B. Malone, who died in 1989, is passed under the large rock at the end of this ridge.)

Every step brings finer and finer views, looking back NE to White Hill and Djouce, separated by the saddle you have crossed, or ahead to the great crag of Fancy (or Luggala) Mountain (where many rock climbing routes have been worked out), or high above to the scree slopes on Lough Tay's shores, the jewel of these hills. From a large rock at the end of the ridge, the Way goes down SSW to the forest corner. It turns left, keeping close to the trees, before entering a tunnel through the trees to the corner of a fence. Keeping the fence on your left, walk the 100m to cross a stile and go right to the forest road, which brings you to the usual barrier as well as a gate and stile into a forest car park (B, Sketch 17) beside the tarmac road R759, sited to give a magnificent view over Lough Tay. You are on a tarmac road for the next 1.5km, so watch the traffic, especially at holiday weekends, though the views ahead (and all around) will claim attention. Traffic-free walking starts again when you leave R759 at a forest entrance (A, Sketch 18), the start of a forest section high upon the east flanks of Sleamaine, whose name means 'the middle mountain', as shown on O.S. Sheet 56. The trees are mostly young, the forest roads are mostly made extra wide, and there are stretches of open ground, so there are wide views. Make sure not to miss the junction (A, Sketch 19), where the trail goes uphill, to the right. Then shortly after this comes a view SW to the cliffs of Tonelagee Mountain, the third highest mountain in Wicklow. The next vital junction is where the road reaches a turntable (B, Sketch 20), and goes on, becoming much narrower and more enclosed by trees, dropping slightly and curving left to eastward.

About 230m from the turntable, turn right by a path on a narrow ride line, which leads SW to a turntable at the edge of the forest (E,

Sketch 20

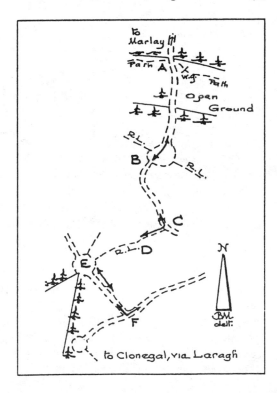

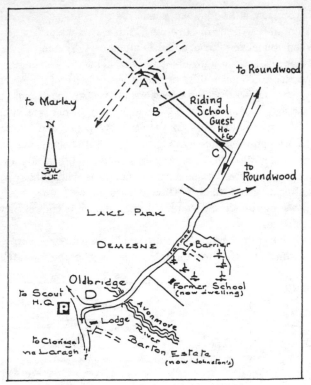

Sketch 20). The view is the excuse for a halt here, where most of
Lough Dan is seen below to westward, backed by Scarr Mountain
and the Cleevaun range, backbone of Wicklow.

From turntable E, the Way goes SE, turns left at the next junction
(F, Sketch 20) and then turns right (A, Sketch 21) to curve to the
right to reach the edge of the forest (B, Sketch 21), and a lane.
Continue down this lane, passing a riding school (care is advisable
here) and a guest house. You will shortly come out to the tarmac
road (C, Sketch 21).

At this point, if you wish to go to Roundwood turn left at the junction,
after covering 20.5km on your second day. Roundwood is now 2.5km
away eastwards, tarmac all the way, mainly downhill, turning right at
the next junction, then left for the final descent to the villlage, which has
accommodation, shops and a twice-daily bus service (St Kevin's)
– the last privately-owned service in the Dublin-Wicklow area.

VARIATIONS

Variation One: Djouce Summit

Distance: 2.5km (extra)   *Time*: 2 hours (extra)

Djouce Mountain (724m), is only about 1km north of the Way, when you have reached the saddle-crest at 640m (Sketch 16).

Djouce is the highest point east of the Sally Gap, offering wonderful views over Central Wicklow, WNW to Kildare and south to the Wexford border. The top is marked by a survey pillar, and by the outcrops called the Three Stones of Djouce, revealing the fact that this is really two mountains in one, with mica schist shoulders eastward, granite to westward – the latter more compact, giving wetter ground with sedges.

You return to the Way by the same route, but for variety White Hill can be by-passed by a sheep track on the west flank, rejoining the Way at or near the gap in the forest fence (A, Sketch 17).

Shorter Walks – Day Two Area

(Knockree-Roundwood)

1. Short Circuit from Crone

Distance: 4.5km   *Time*: 1½-2 hours

Route Outline   Crone Car Park (Sketch 13) – Forest Road/Wicklow Way – Crone Car Park.

This is a short ramble for motorists using Crone Forest car park (Sketch 13) in Glencree, reached from Enniskerry via Tinnahinch Bridge, on the road from the village to Powerscourt Waterfall.

The road drops sharply towards the Waterfall Gate (O 207 133) but leave this alone, keeping to the public road for a further 1.5km, when Crone car park entrance comes up on the left.

Having safely parked, go straight ahead at the barrier, walking on a rather up-and-down forest road, heading roughly west, through young trees which have replaced mature ones, this being one of the most successful plantings in these mountains (begun before 1930).

The road rises to a T-junction at which you turn right. In a few moments you come to unplanted ground on either side, for this road is a link between two separate plantings – Maulin Forest, now behind you and Ballyreagh Wood, straight ahead, mantling the slopes of massive Tonduff.

The view on your right covers middle Glencree, with the isolated Knockree, a hill whose name bemused one of the pioneers of Celtic studies, a certain General Vallency, back before 1800. The gallant general thought that this was 'The hill of the King' (*Cnoc an Rí*) and that the whole structure of soil and rock, of field and forest, had been piled up by the ancient Irish as a basis for a palace for the local monarch. To which one can only say: Some earth moving, some monarch! It is, of course, a natural formation.

Keep straight on at the next junction with a grassy track to the left and the road brings you on west through the lower parts of Ballyreagh Wood, which was once part of the Powerscourt Estate, planted before 1870 when the Lord Powerscourt of the time put two million trees here. Hardly anything of the original planting survives, thanks to sundry storms, a serious fire, and the demands of two world wars; but state forestry took over years ago, so replanting goes steadily on.

I suggest that you about-turn at the next road fork (O 178 146) and go back along the route you have come to the fork in Maulin Forest.

You now follow the forest road on the right back across the lower flanks of Maulin, keeping left and enjoying views ahead to Great Sugar Loaf Mountain before the road drops to a junction with the Way (B, Sketch 13). Here you go down left, following the Way. As you approach the map board, a path cuts the corner, going right down to the entrance and to your parked car in Crone car park.

2. *A Short Classic: Crone Car Park – Lake Car Park*

Distance: 6.5km   *Time*: 2½-3 hours

Route Outline   Crone Car Park – Ride Rock – Watergates Ford/Bridge – Corner Deerpark Wall – Forest Roads – Lake Car Park.

This is a classic walk from car park to car park; it needs a car at both ends, or a non-walking driver, prepared to drive around to await the walkers' arrival at Lake car park (O 210 113).

The route was a 'Wilderness Trek Trail', set up by the forestry, and marked by white posts, quite a while before Cospoir set up the Wicklow Way (almost all trace of those white posts has vanished now).

From Crone, go up to join the Way at B, Sketch 13, and follow same on, over the Watergates Ford (B, Sketch 15), then uphill, with the old Deerpark stone wall and the fence of the forest on your left hand.

The Wicklow Way goes round the corner of the forest fence, continuing uphill and here you leave the Way, crossing the fence by a stile only a couple of metres from the corner post. (For crossing fences without stiles, experienced walkers carry a very battered rain cape or even a pair of old socks, which are laid on or draped over the wire to prevent accidents. Remember also that if a fence or gate is to be crossed, only one person at a time should be crossing it, as nothing wrecks a fence or gate faster than three or four people hanging out of it.) Once inside the fence, standing with your back to it, head up diagonally right, over unplanted, dry, but tussocky ground, till on your right, at a projecting corner of trees, you will see a forest road on the right, which will lead you almost directly down to the Lake car park.

The first landmark is a 300m stretch, which, after rain, is often very muddy, so that you have to walk on the road banks. Then comes a forest crossroads (keep straight ahead), and about a kilometre later the well-surfaced road curves left and descends to leave you almost alongside the dam of the former Paddock Pond (O 208 113). Until 'Hurricane Charlie' struck in 1986, this was an attractive ornamental lake, which also supplied power for a saw mill below in the Deerpark, and was built for Lord Powerscourt by Thomas Parnell, an uncle of the late nineteenth-century Irish leader, Charles Stewart Parnell. Speaking of Thomas, Lord Powerscourt plaintively remarked, 'How much more useful was his work, than that of his nephew, the agitator!' The 1986 hurricane put paid to poor Thomas' work, ripping the middle out of the dam, which is now restored; but the sluice controls have vanished so the pond is now floored with rushes and vegetation.

Across the dam turn right and go south, with the rushes on your right, to where the path goes up to the left by the edge of the forest, leading to the Lake car park and your transport.

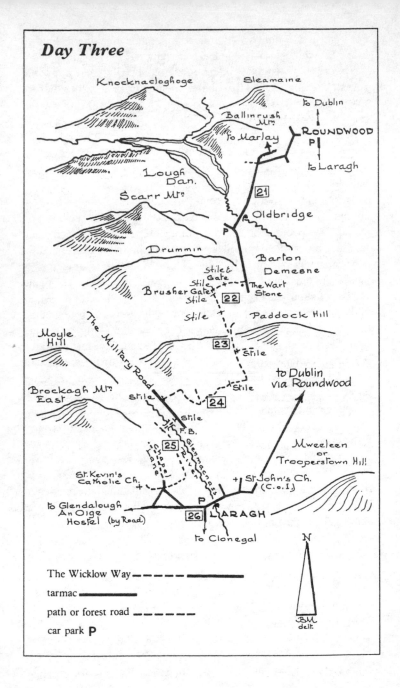

Day Three

Knocknacloghoge

Sleamaine

to Dublin

Ballinrush Mtn

to Marlay

ROUNDWOOD P

to Laragh

21

Oldbridge

P

Barton Demesne

Lough Dan.

Scarr Mtn

Drummin

Stile & Gate

Stile

Brusher Gate

Stile

22

The Wart Stone

Stile

Paddock Hill

The Military Road

Moyle Hill

23

Stile

Brockagh Mtn East

Stile

Stile

24

to Dublin via Roundwood

Stile

Glenmacnass River

F.B.

25

Mweeleen or Trooperstown Hill

St. Kevin's Catholic Ch.

St John's Ch. (C.o.I.)

to Glendalough An Oige Hostel (by Road)

P

26 **LARAGH**

to Clonegal

N

The Wicklow Way — — — ——

tarmac ——————

path or forest road — — — — —

car park **P**

BM delt.

62

Day Three . The Third Walk

Roundwood to Laragh/Glendalough

Distance: 10km   *Time*: 4-5 hours

Route Outline   Roundwood – Lake Park Crossroads – Oldbridge – Brusher Gate Boreen – Paddock Hill Forest Firebreak – Glenmacnass Forest (part of) – Military Road – Mass Path Footbridge – Laragh Village.

Parking   Roundwood – Oldbridge (D, Sketch 21) – Glenmacnass Forest Entrance – Brockagh Forest Entrance – Laragh Village.

A walker could hardly ask better than to be starting early from Roundwood, with bright clear weather, an easy day ahead, short in distance, lacking any great hardship.

From Roundwood go back past Lake Park crossroads to head SW on the tarmac road.

On the way up from Roundwood, the views east show the two Vartry ponds, as these reservoirs are locally known. The right-hand pond (1863) was the original Dublin water supply, the left hand being the Vartry Extension (1923); both were added to in 1939, when the Poulaphouca water scheme (in West Wicklow) brought water to the city.

The Vartry water is so pure it is claimed that even coming through Dublin taps it can be used for any purpose for which distilled water is needed – in fact, your real Dubliner will never put anything into whiskey except a small drop of Vartry water.

Discussing these and similar intriguing topics will have brought you to the descent towards Oldbridge, a bridge over the Avonmore River. The woods of Lake Park are on the right, state forest on the left, with two landmarks also on the left – the forest entrance and a former schoolhouse, now a dwelling for several years but still marked 'Sch' on some maps.

Oldbridge, just downstream of Lough Dan, is a concrete structure dating from about 1934, replacing a bridge of 1823, of which only a dated stone survives, built into the eastern parapet wall of the present bridge at the northern end.

Next, at a T-junction (D, Sketch 21), go left, uphill, with the pine trees and stone walling of the former Barton Estate on the left and no more than a glimpse of Lough Dan behind you. This estate belonged to a Mr Hugo in 1798. He was very active against the Irish rebels, and on his land was a tree (the 'murdering tree', long since felled) against which Hugo was alleged to have shot his victims. Sure enough, when the tree was cut down the trunk was found to be full of bullets – at just about the height of a person.

Just 2.5km of tarmac road from Oldbridge brings you to the turn for a gate known as the Brusher Gate (A, Sketch 22).

The Wart Stone field is on the left after you turn off right (west) from the road. It is named from a stone with a deep hollow in it, possibly a primitive handmill. The water gathered in the hollow was reputed to be a certain cure for warts. These hollowed-out stones (*bullauns*) are especially plentiful around Glendalough, and seem to be associated with early Christian sites, hermitages perhaps, or outfarms of a large monastery. The historian Liam Price made the intriguing suggestion that bullauns were introduced by Christian refugees from Roman Britain, when the pagan Saxons arrived, and the *bullauns* themselves were used in the making of altar bread; hence the reverence they were accorded till quite recently. After crossing the stile at the second gate, you turn left, immediately crossing another stile, to head south on a path on a forest firebreak (B, Sketch 22), the trees here being part of fairly recent planting in Drummin townland.

The Brusher Gate, which you left behind at the end of the boreen, is traditionally the place where local people left food for the nineteenth-century rebel Michael Dwyer and his men, who held out in the recesses of these mountains for some five years after the quelling of Irish resistance in Wexford following the uprising of 1798. There are wide views east on this section, over the glen of the Avonmore River to forested Castlekevin Hill (294m), and its southerly neighbours, Moneystown (386m), and Trooperstown Hill (known locally as Mweeleen) (430m).

These eastern heights, being isolated from the main mountains, give memorable views on clear days. Drummin Forest firebreak ends at C (Sketches 22, 23) but the Way goes on south, over ferny ground, ignoring a rutted path going east down to the same road you left in favour of the Brusher Gate boreen (C, Sketch 22). Now

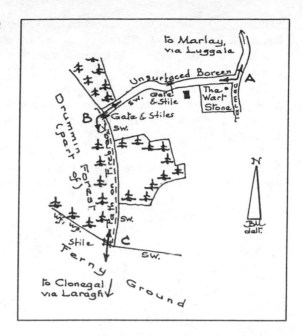

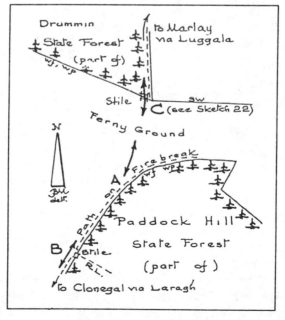

you avoid losing height, and join another firebreak path (A, Sketch 23), this time above Paddock Hill Forest, leading on SSW. The next landmark is a stile in the forest fence on the left, a good place to halt and admire the western view (B, Sketch 23).

The foreground is all bare moorland, scrubby heather and grazings, with scattered rocks, displaying plenty of white quartzite. Above the unseen depths of Glenmacnass Valley Tonelagee Mountain (817m) rears, a wall of cliffs above hidden Lough Ouler – cliffs already seen distantly from Sleamaine Mountain, but seen here from a more southerly angle, showing their giant structure of rock rib and buttress. Due west, Brockagh Mountain is revealed as

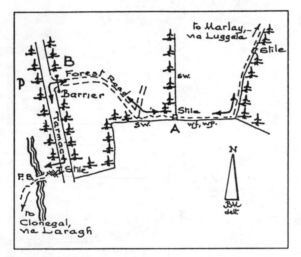

Sketch 24

an almost independent satellite of Tonelagee. The less shapely summit to the NW is Moyle (called Mall Hill on some maps). Going on south, the Way drops south towards Laragh, then turns right, to cross a stile at the SE corner of forestry in Glenmacnass (A, Sketch 24). From the stile a path and a forest road lead down to the Military Road (B, Sketch 24). The steep path twists down through the trees, keeping fairly close to the edge of the forest, then it meets a forest road at an elbow and goes down to the gate and barrier, turning left on meeting the Military Road.

This is the highest through road, and one of the most interesting, in Ireland. We owe this road to the rebel leaders Michael Dwyer and Robert Emmet (uprisings of 1798 and 1803 respectively)

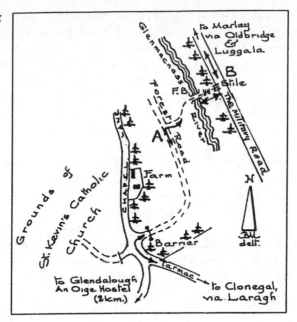

whose rapid movements through these mountains so alarmed Dublin Castle authorities that it was speedily decided that 'something must be done!' Accordingly, around 1800, a Highland regiment was put to work here (for a shilling a day) and perhaps the grandsons of men who marched with the Jacobite Prince Charles Edward Stuart (affectionately known as the 'Bonnie Prince') in 1745, laboured here to give us this Military Road.

Presumably paperwork played its usual role in slowing the rate of construction, for Emmet was already in his grave and Dwyer transported across the seas into exile before the job was finished and the 'Redcoat' Crown soldiers could march in comparative ease from end to end of Wicklow, with stout barracks en route at Glencree, Laragh, Drumgoff and Aghavannagh.

About 270m further south, turn right, over a stile (B, Sketch 25) to follow a mass path over the Glenmacnass Footbridge, towards Laragh Catholic church.

Once common in Ireland, mass paths, like sundry other aspects of religion, have had to face the combined assault of technology and affluence, for even the most pious parishioner will not trek two miles when he can be whisked in comfort in his own or in a neighbour's car to the church in a quarter of the time.

Mass paths are relics of an earlier time when almost every country person walked, and only the gentry and the strongest of strong farmers owned a riding horse. Walking would have been the normal way of travel, to markets, to small village shops, to cross the hill to borrow a scythe, or court a neighbour's daughter. Before Catholic Emancipation in 1829 which ended the Penal laws by which Catholic worship was outlawed, Catholic churches were built well away from the main roads. In fact, even up to about 1870, some of the more bigoted landlords insisted that places of Papist worship be kept outside the towns they controlled.

Similarly, schoolpaths from farms to the schoolhouse also fell into disuse when school buses started to collect the pupils.

By this attractive mass path you come over to a forest road (A, Sketch 25), turning left onto it for Laragh.

At the forest gate, continue straight and turn left at the gate of St Kevin's Church if making for accommodation at Glendalough An Oige Hostel, although it may be preferable to proceed on to the fourth day's walk and leave the route near the monastic ruins for the hostel; otherwise turn left for a selection of accommodation in Laragh (Sketch 26).

If you have started reasonably early from Roundwood, you will have a half day left to explore historic Glendalough, the round tower, the seven churches (not forgetting St Saviour's, the most highly decorated of all), the twin lakes, the interpretative centre, and perhaps even the isolated Van Dieman's mines, high above the Upper Lough. The fourth day's route will be passing all of these (except Van Dieman's mines) but there may not be time available to visit them, as the distance to be covered is 29km.

VARIATIONS

Variation One: Roundwood to Laragh via Annamoe
Distance: 7km   *Time*: 2½-3 hours

Motorists will have to park their cars at Annamoe and depend on a non-walking driver to take the car on to Laragh (5km). Alternatively, you could take the St Kevin's Bus to Annamoe from Roundwood.

From the centre of Annamoe village backtrack east over the bridge, turn right, and about 200m further on, fork downhill to the right to cross a small stone bridge (T 177 987), with Castlekevin Hill rising SSE before you. Looking east from the bridge, you will notice a green mound above the yellow-brown wastes of rushes and sedge that cumber the ground. This mound has every look of a *crannóg* – a lake dwelling commonly found in Ireland and probably dating from the Iron Age. Such dwellings were probably built for security. This mound has never been excavated, but there is no doubt that these rushy levels, stretching away east, were a great lake after the Ice Age and would have offered a safe refuge for early settlers.

A scheme by the Electricity Supply Board to flood this ancient lake-bed again for a hydro-electric scheme by means of dam building, only got as far as the drawing board some time after the Second World War.

South of the stone bridge, you meet a T-junction and go right (T 177 986), but first throw a glance left, to the stone-pillared entrance to Castlekevin House. This was once owned by relatives of J.M. Synge, poet and playwright, who often stayed here. It has been said that Synge's own bedroom was directly over the kitchen, and that through a knot-hole, he heard the conversation of the servants, which helped him to create the colourful speech and turn of phrase used afterwards in *The Playboy of the Western World* and other works. If this is true then these servants must have come from the West of Ireland as the speech patterns he used in his plays are definitely western. It should also be noted that this knot-hole story has also been told of other Wicklow houses!

The right turn at Castlekevin House entrance passes a fork on the right to a private house then it enters gates and becomes a forest road. Continue along this forest road around the base of Castlekevin Hill, passing a road from the left, then one from the right. The place invites dawdling as the trail passes beneath mature oaks, beeches and birches, and there are bluebells and fraughans, in their seasons. The fraughan is a many-named fruit, like a tiny grape, also called blaeberries, bilberries, whortleberries, whorts and hurts in different parts of the country.

Ahead now, the road ends at a rather overgrown (or unfinished?) forest turntable, but you head briefly SSW to a small plank bridge over the streamlet from Trooperstown Hill. This bridge (T 168 970) is slightly upstream of the position given for it on some maps.

The road continues to pass through a forest barrier and crosses the stream from Trooperstown Hill by a concrete bridge. On the south bank the usual conifers replace the birches. The next landmark is a T-junction (go right here), and at a second T-junction go right again to cross a bridge over the Avonmore River (or cross the river by the stepping stones, if preferred), from which the road leads up NW to join the busy R755 (the Dublin- Roundwood-Laragh road), at a forest entrance (T 156 972). Again you go right, keeping well in to the right side, for some 200m, then cross to turn left onto a forest road, with the usual barrier, leading up to the Oldbridge-Laragh road. Straight ahead is another forest barrier; past this the forest road turns north and passes a road in from the left. After about 100m you fork left onto a ride line, the second of two close together which are beyond the corner of a field on the right. Cross a track rising to reach a stile (B, Sketch 23). Here you go left, joining the main route via the footbridge and mass path to Laragh.

Shorter Walk – *Day Three Area (Roundwood-Glendalough)*

1 *Wide Views, Slight Effort: Laragh*

Distance: 6km   *Time*: 2½-3½ hours

Route Outline Laragh – Oldbridge Road – Paddock Hill – Forest Entrance – Stile – Wicklow Way – Laragh.

Motorists park in Laragh for this rewarding but by no means difficult circuit. The walk starts by crossing Laragh Bridge (Sketch 26) then taking the second turn left from the Dublin Road – this turn has a sign indicating St John's Church (Church of Ireland). This is on your left as you go uphill, a dark, plain Gothic building with tower, while also on the left, a few moments later, you see the bastion of Laragh Castle wall, almost on the roadside. This was originally Laragh Barracks, built about 1803 as part of the chain of barracks linked by the Military Road. Still climbing, you pass several modern bungalows, where the road gives wide views to your right, looking east and SE toward Trooperstown Hill and the summits above the Vale of Clara.

Next, the road levels off between two forests, and two forest entrance barriers appear. Take the entrance on the left, walking on a forest road that soon swings right. Before long you pass a forest road in from the left and beyond the corner of a field behind the trees on the right take a wide line (the second of two close together) to the left, starting parallel to the forest road and then rising to cross a track and reach a stile (B, Sketch 23).

If you have a fine clear day it is worth strolling out for five minutes from the stile to look out over Glenmacnass to the high mountains that are the backbone of Wicklow, dividing the westward-flowing rivers from those that go more directly to the Irish Sea.

There is a local story that many years back, when the Barton Estate included almost all Glenmacnass, a local man rented the grazing on this side of Scarr Mountain (O 132 018), about 4km north of where you now stand. The story goes that Mr Barton asked the sheepman to keep an eye out for any signs of valuable minerals and a long while after, the same man stumbled on a vein of lead 'as thick as your arm'. Realising that if a rich lead mine opened, his grazing days were over, the sheepman hastily covered up the offending vein with earth and stones. Even on his deathbed he never revealed the exact location to anyone, so the lost lead mine remains a mystery to this day.

Returning to the stile (B, Sketch 23), follow the Way (by Sketches 24, 25, 26) back to Laragh and your car.

Sketch 26

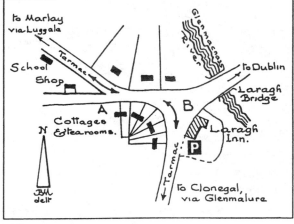

71

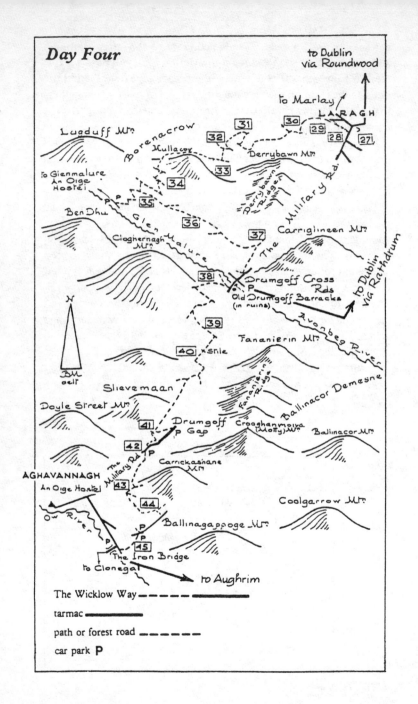

Day Four

to Dublin
via Roundwood

to Marlay

LARAGH

Lugduff Mtn.

Borenacrow

Mullacor

31

32

30

29 28 27

Derrybawn Mtn.

33

34

Derrybawn Ridge

to Glenmalure
An Oige
Hostel

P 35

Ben Dhu

Glen

36

37

Carriglineen Mtn.

The Military Rd.

to Dublin via Rathdrum

Cloghernagh
Mtn.

Malure

38

Drumgoff Cross
Rds
P

N

Old Drumgoff Barracks
(in ruins)

Avonbeg River

39

Fananierin Mtn.

BM
0617

40 stile

Slievemaan

Fananierin Rd.

Ballinacor Demesne

Doyle Street Mtn.

41

Drumgoff
P Gap

Crooghanmoira
(Motty) Mtn.

Ballinacor Mtn.

42 P

Carrickashane
Mtn.

AGHAVANNAGH

The Military Rd.

43

Coolgarrow Mtn.

An Oige Hostel

44

Ow River

P

P 45

Ballinagappoge Mtn.

The Iron Bridge

to Clonegal

to Aughrim

The Wicklow Way — — — — —

tarmac ———————

path or forest road — — — — —

car park P

72

Day Four . The Fourth Walk

Laragh/Glendalough to Aghavannagh An Oige Hostel

Distance: 32km   *Time*: 8-9 hours.

Route Outline   Laragh – Green Road to Glendalough – Derrybawn Forest Tracks – Borenacrow – Drumgoff Crossroads – Cloghernagh Forest Tracks – Drumgoff Gap – Carrickashane Forest Tracks – Iron Bridge – Aghavannagh Hostel.

Parking   Laragh – Glendalough (Visitors' Centre, free, variable opening hours) – Glendalough (Lower Car Park, free) – Glendalough (Upper Lake, fee payable) – Coolalingo Bridge – Drumgoff Crossroads (Glenmalure Lodge) – Drumgoff Gap (Forest Entrance) – Carrickashane Forest Entrance (A, Sketch 42) – Forest Entrance, Brown Mount Road – Iron Bridge Picnic Site (A, Sketch 46).

The fourth day on the Wicklow Way is, in at least one way, one of the high points of the whole tour for, crossing Borenacrow, you are, at 550m, at one of the loftiest points on the Way. Also, the scenery is really spectacular almost all day. This is not to say that the rest of the route is dull, but it has a gentler charm, running through lower hill, more wooded and pastoral.

Starting from Laragh, go south on the Rathdrum road, turning right after less than a kilometre along the entrance to the Woollen Mills (Sketch 27). Continue across the bridge, through the arch and courtyard (A, Sketch 27), past the Independent Hostel on to a Green Road which keeps more or less parallel to the river (Sketch 28). You pass on the right (A, Sketch 28), now deep in forest, the ruins of St Saviour's, the most highly decorated of all the Glendalough churches, as well as the entrances to the visitor centre (B, Sketch 28) and to the renowned monastic ruins (C, Sketch 28). A visit to these is highly recommended. The An Oige youth hostel can also be approached from here. Next comes the reedy shore of the Lower Lake and the jagged rocky face of the Giant's Cut. All the while, there are the most delightful views of the lovely valley with the

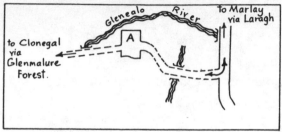

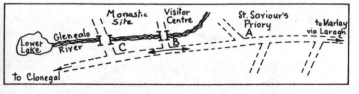

steep mountainsides on the other side and the lower forested steep side of Derrybawn on your left.

Continue to the information centre and turn left across a bridge (A, Sketch 29) up the steep slope past Pollanass Waterfall, a well-known beauty spot. A main forest road is joined shortly (B, Sketch 29) and then you turn left following the track across two bridges. Fork right at the next junction (D, Sketch 29), climbing steadily to reach another main forest road. Before turning right (A, Sketch 30) to follow the route, it is worth going forward for a short distance to enjoy the wonderful view. Here the whole setting of Glendalough is revealed: the Upper Lough beneath the hanging valley of Glenaflagh, which is held between the narrow ridge of Lugduff Spink and the majestic bulk of Camaderry Mountain to northward, its ranges of cliffs plunging almost to the lakeshore. Looking further to the left, SW, you see the dome of Mullacor Mountain rising to 657m, above a complex of forested ridges, and to the right of Mullacor, the skyline ridge sloping down to the pass of Borenacrow, which the Way crosses to get to Glenmalure. Thanks to forestry roads and ride lines, the task is not so toilsome at all. First follow the forest road south, crossing the concrete bridge over Lugduff stream, then fork right (A, Sketch 31), to drop and swing right over the Pollanass stream, then rise to join another forest road (B, Sketch 31).

A long gradual rise brings you close under the ridge of Mullacor, then the road curves left to Junction C, Sketch 32 in an area of

Sketch 29

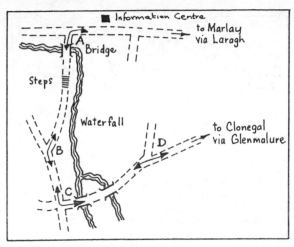

Sketch 30

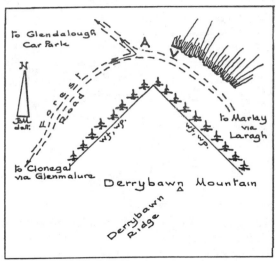

younger trees where only handfuls of older trees survive.

Borenacrow, as a pass, goes back to ancient times. There was a tradition in Glenmalure that St Kevin (about A.D. 600) came this way to say mass in the glen, this being almost the only place where the crossing can be made without meeting cliffs.

The view from Borenacrow, though less wide than from the tops on either side of the pass, has subtle 'extras', more detail of the Fraughan Rock Glen, south of Glenmalure, and a better view of the Stoney Road

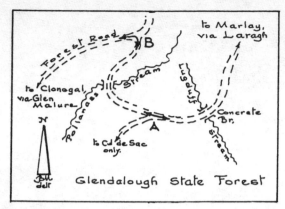

Sketch 31

Glendalough State Forest

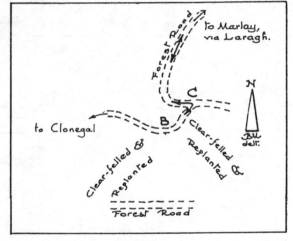

Sketch 32

climbing the glen head, and of the cliffs above Art's Lough (T 057 931).

When the path starts to drop south, you can either slant off left (to B, Sketch 33), or go ahead to the much-gapped fence, then turn left to head straight on SSE for about 400m to a projecting corner of trees, where a ride line brings you down right, and you turn left over a stone ramp, at a forest road (C, Sketch 34).

The only snag on the next 5km is that you are heading SE, down Glenmalure, with your back to the majestic massif of Lugnacullia, but there are still great views before you, apart from the graceful outline of Croaghanmoira ahead to SE (T 099 865).

At junction D (Sketch 34) you look west up Glenmalure to see the great rock-ribs of Ben Leagh Mountain revealed by the

Sketch 33

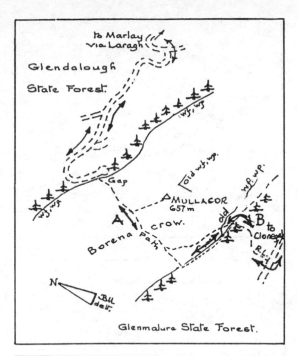

Sketch 34

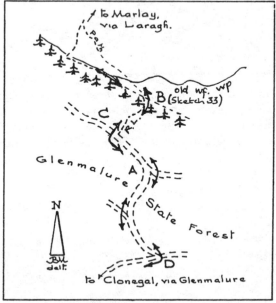

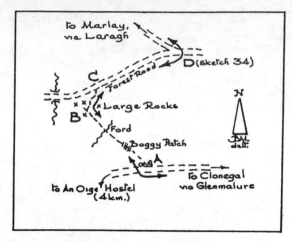

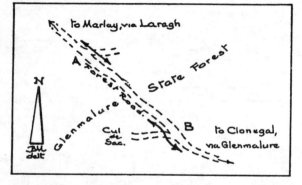

sunlight. Then you take a path through rocks which before the area was felled, left you deep in forest on a grassy path (nicknamed the 'tunnel of love' by some Dublin walkers). Built to serve long-abandoned mines, this path has a minor ford on a streamlet, then a small boggy patch before you come through a screen of bushes to a forest road (A, Sketch 35).

Here you at last see the floor of Glenmalure valley, the foaming and flashing Avonbeg River, and the full height of the mountain wall, south of the glen.

Here also those making for Glenmalure An Oige Hostel turn off to the right by a zigzag road, soon becoming a track, which begins as a sharp hairpin bend right as you reach the debris from a landslide in 1934.

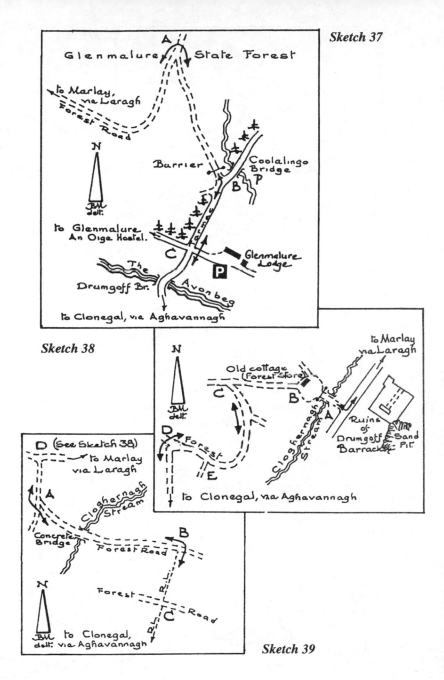

Sketch 37

Glenmalure State Forest

to Marlay, na Laragh

Forest Road

N
BM delt:

Barrier

Coolalingo Bridge

B P

to Glenmalure An Oige Hostel.

C

The Drumgoff Br.

Avonbeg

P

Glenmalure Lodge

to Clonegal, via Aghavannagh

Sketch 38

N
BM delt:

Old cottage (Forest Store)

C

B

D

Forest

E

Cloghernagh Stream

A

to Marlay na Laragh

Ruins of Drumgoff Barracks

Sand Pit

to Clonegal, via Aghavannagh

D (See Sketch 38)

to Marlay via Laragh

A

Cloghernagh Stream

Concrete Bridge

Forest Road

B

Forest

R.L.

Road

C

N
BM delt:

to Clonegal, via Aghavannagh

Sketch 39

79

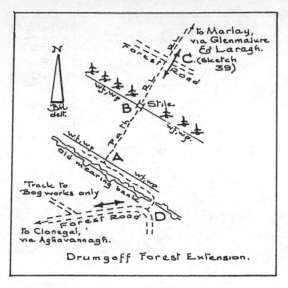

To Marlay, via Glenmalure & Laragh.
C. (Sketch 39)

Forest Road

Stile

B

N

B.M. delt.

A

Track to Bog works only

To Clonegal, via Aghavannagh.

Forest Road

D

Drumgoff Forest Extension.

The track zigzags down to a car park (T 081 937). The hostel is reached by turning right on a tarmac road, 3km NW, up the glen (check current *An Oige Handbook* for opening days for this hostel).

The main Way goes on towards Drumgoff crossroads, on a fairly level forest road; only two junctions are passed (Sketch 36), but there are endless views across the glen. The trail passes above landslide debris. Local legend says that a man found a sizeable gold nugget down on the road after the slide. Further SE, there is a grandstand view of Carrawaystick Waterfall (T 085 918), beside a zigzag track leading up to long-abandoned bog workings on the south side of the glen. The road begins to curve left (Sketch 37) and you see Carriglineen Mountain (T 118 911) rising ahead, all forest, little rock faces and lofty grazings, towering above Drumgoff crossroads, above the Avonbeg River and the ruined barracks. The Way now descends rapidly, makes a hairpin turn SSE (A, Sketch 37), dropping to join a tarmac road at Coolalingo Bridge (B, Sketch 37), and keeps on SW at Drumgoff crossroads (C, Sketch 37).

The notice board, warning of artillery ranges in glaring red and white at the crossroads, is intended to deter travellers from going up Glenmalure, up over the Stoney Road, and down almost in the middle of the artillery ranges which occupy the NE corner of the Glen of Imaal, but the ugly board is too far from the scene of action

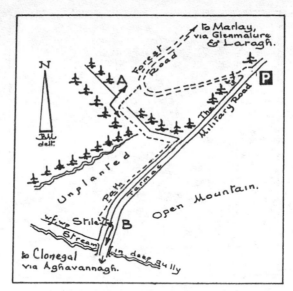

in any case and of course is not relevant to the Way.

Next, on the left, the battered shell of Drumgoff Barracks is seen. A military 'folly' if ever there was one, these ruins prove that truth is always the first casualty in war, even when long-past military history comes to be written. After 1950, a work in weekly parts came out with a photo of these ruins which, it was stated, were burnt by nationalist republican Sinn Féiners in 1920, during a campaign against Royal Irish Constabulary barracks. In actual fact, Drumgoff has been quietly crumbling to ruin since 1820, when the 'Redcoats' left, and the destruction has been greatly helped by sandpit workings, which have broken down the SE corner of the enceinte.

Here the Way turns right (A, Sketch 38), to zigzag up part of Cloghernagh Mountain. On the first sharp bend left as you climb with another aspect of Glenmalure spread before you, not only the views suggest a halt: you may rest with a sense of achievement if you are doing the complete Way, for you are now just over 65.5km from its start in Marlay Park and half your journey to Clonegal is behind you. Turning left (east) and running fairly level (D, Sketch 38) you change maps, walking off O.S. Sheet 56 and onto Sheet 52.

Look out for a ride line going up to the right, heading SW (B, Sketch 39). Following this ride line you cross a forest road, climb straight up to a stile, now unsafe and bypassed, then level off (A,

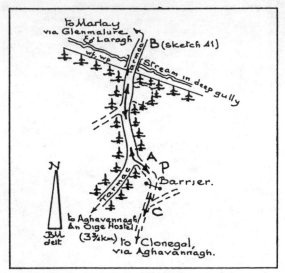

Sketch 40) before reaching the 'elbow' of a forest road (D, Sketch 40).

Now comes about 2.5km of easy going on a forest road, wide enough to give views back northward over most of the Way previously traversed, back over the Glenmalure and Glendalough mountains, right back to Djouce and Great Sugar Loaf Mountains.

Also to eastward there are views of Croaghanmoira, locally called the Motty Mountain, probably from its peaked outline – a 'motty' being a mark at which horseshoes or quoits were thrown.

Also impressive is the view of Fananierin ridge striking northerly from the Motty, while looking further ahead, to SSE, the crests of Carrickashane and other southern satellites of Croaghanmoira rise up, showing that only one more mountain barrier has to be crossed to get to Aghavannagh Hostel.

Sketch 41 shows how the Way quits the forest road and at length reaches a tarmac road. The path just west of the forest fence avoids traffic; it also gives views into West Wicklow, to the long, even ridge of Slieve Margy Mountain on the borders of counties Carlow and Kilkenny. Prominent in the plains is the sharp outline of the Hump of Hacketstown, also called Eagle Hill. Cross the stile (B, Sketch 41), turning right onto the tarmac road.

After about 300m, forest begins on the left. Look for a forest entrance (A, Sketch 42) with a barrier hidden round a corner, after which you head straight up the western flank of Carrickashane

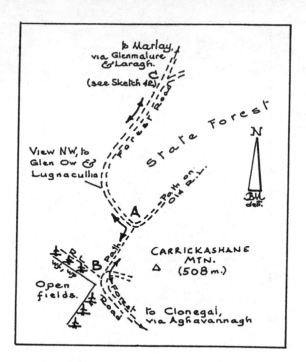

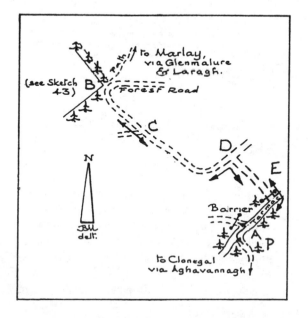

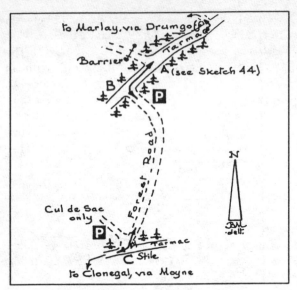

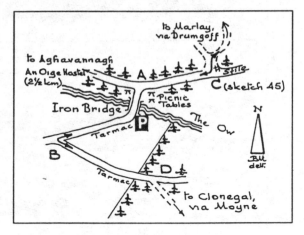

Mountain, 508m. The forest road brings you up to about 450m, with views west over Glen Ow, showing the great South Prison cliffs of 'Lug' (as Lugnacullia is familiarly known), which dominate all neighbouring tops. Ahead to southward rise prominent hills, like Shielstown, through which the Way rolls on to Clonegal.

Junction A, Sketch 43, now comes up where a turn right, on a path, leads down nearly due west. This is a narrow ride line between trees: mature trees on the right and younger ones on the left.

You now reach a sort of forest crossroads (B, Sketch 43). The Way goes downhill here, gradually levelling off, with an overgrown forest road coming in on the right (C, Sketch 44). Continue on the forest road as it descends gradually and curves left. At the T-junction go right to descend to a barrier, where you turn right on a tarmac road at a stile (C, Sketch 46). This steep forest road has not been improved by its use as a timber slide. After felling, the ground in forests is often left cluttered with debris and among the stumps and broken branches new planting is done. Forestry Service officials intend the debris to rot down and thus fertilise new growth, and the jagged branches deter sheep from rambling through these slopes and perhaps damaging the young trees. The visual effect close-up is certainly one of dire devastation.

At Junction A (Sketch 46), do not cross to the Iron Bridge if you are going to Aghavannagh Hostel. Instead, keep straight ahead on a rising road, levelling off after a junction (T 069 850), then go left at a T-junction (T 065 861) for the final half kilometre, to the tall old building standing out clearly to the right of the road, built about 1804 as part of the chain of barracks linked by the Military Road.

VARIATIONS

Variation One: Mullacor Summit

Distance: 1.5km (extra) *Time*: 1 hour (extra)

Mullacor Mountain, 657m, is just over half a kilometre SE of the Way when you have reached the saddle at Borenacrow and was at one time included in it.

No cairn, no rock outcrop marks the fairly squelchy, sedgy gound of Mullacor top, only the remnants of a wire fence on wooden posts and a bog pool, both east of the top (Sketch). Here in clear weather, you get the finest views of Wicklow's finest glens.

Northward, you look over the forested ridge of Lugduff Spink to where Camaderry Mountain rises above Glendalough, while more to the right are the round tower and the seven churches of Glendalough.

NW of you is Lugduff, backed by the dome of aptly-named

Conavalla, 'Head of the Road' mountain, left of which you see the white thread of the Stoney Road (T 030 064) climbing to the skyline of Glenmalure. From WNW to SSE mountains fill the horizon, with Lugnacullia Mountain (on O.S. maps spelt Lugnaquilla) lifting above all to 925m, the highest point in Leinster, in fact higher than any point in Ireland outside Kerry.

You return to the Way by the same route, rejoining it in the saddle of Borenacrow and turning left (Sketch 33) to continue the journey southwards.

Shorter Walks – *Day Four*

(Laragh-Aghavannagh)

1. *Above the Trail: Mullacor*

Distance: 8km   *Time*: 2½-3½ hours

Route Outline   Logra13nia (Glenmalure) Car Park – Wicklow Way – Mullacor Summit – same route down – Logra13nia Car Park.

Mullacor (657m), is easily accessible from the Wicklow Way, and is well worth reaching for its own sake.

Motorists park at the forest car park near Logra13nia (T 081 927), which is about 3.5km up Glenmalure, from Drumgoff crossroads, on the right. At the back of the parking area, almost at the foot of a cascade, a deteriorating log bridge leads you on to an old track, zigzagging up to the long-abandoned Ballinafunshoge Mines, going left in a final zigzag to avoid the mines debris, joining a clear forest road above the mines, where you find yourself on the Wicklow Way, at the bottom of the path between the forest tracks (A, Sketch 35).

From here, follow the Way up to the saddle in Borenacrow, turning right to climb to the top of Mullacor (Sketches 35, 34, 33), and make your descent by the same route.

2. A Glenmalure Grandstand

Distance: 7.5km *Time*: 2½-3½ hours

Route Outline   Forest Entrance, Coolalingo Bridge – Wicklow Way – Forest Road, Ballyboy – Coolalingo Bridge.

If you want a grandstand view of Glenmalure, try this circular walk which involves part of the Way, plus some high-level forest roads.

Park at the double forest entrances beside Coolalingo Bridge (Sketch 37), taking care not to block either track or, if preferred, park opposite the Glenmalure Lodge. Follow the Way as far as junction A (Sketch 36), turning right there to reach an upper road, turning right again. So far, you have enjoyed panoramas of Upper Glenmalure, now you face the lower part of the same glen, wider and showing farms and tillage, but still dominated by shapely mountains.

Keep straight ahead, where a road on the left doubles back up to a still higher road (T 101 915); but your road runs pretty level, curving around Ballyboy Mountain, which is the last outlier of Mullacor.

So you get further grandstand views, this time over the little glen of Braigue (T 115 925 which most maps call Ballybraid, while on your right are views of Carriglineen Mountain, which looks much higher than its 455m.

You next make a hairpin bend down to the right, but do not take the next junction left; instead keep straight on to rejoin the Way, going down to your car at Coolalingo (or at Drumgoff).

3. The Graceful Mountain: Croaghanmoira

Distance: 10km *Time*: 4-5 hours

Being so near the Wicklow Way, the extra fine viewpoint of graceful Croaghanmoira will not be overlooked by keen walkers, whether motorised or not. Cars park at A (Sketch 42) and the Way is followed, only as far as C (Sketch 42). Quit the Way here, turning left to follow a forest road up NE, then curve around to the south. Stay on the road as it climbs, passing a road in from the right, to where it levels off and is crossed by an obvious ride line on both sides of the road. Turn onto the left ride line which leads to the forest fence and firebreak, turning right for the summit itself (664m) and up the final steep rise to the crest, marked by a survey pillar (of 1953 vintage). Given good weather, the view rewards all toil, and you speedily realise why this was a major station in the original Ordnance Survey of Great Britain and Ireland in 1825. Officially put down as 'Ballycreen Hill', this spot saw intense activity for weeks and months, as the sappers dragged up their large, heavy, but accurate theodolites and telescopes and set up their apparatus for making the new-fangled Drummond light. Camping on the top, the surveyors waited weeks to exchange light signals by night with stations as far apart as Precelly (South Wales), Keeper Mountain (Co. Tipperary), Mount Leinster (Co. Carlow) and Galtymore (Co. Tipperary).

In 1953, using the latest electronic aids, there was a re-survey of the principal bearings observed by the men of 1825, but no appreciable error was found in the original work – this has been further confirmed by modern satellite pictures.

The shortest route back to your car is by retracing your line of ascent (making the day's trip 5km, requiring 2 to 3 hours), but it is more interesting to continue on across Croaghanmoira by the firebreak, now almost a road. Where it levels out and veers left take a wide grassy rock-strewn track hard right. Stay on this to Ballingappoga Bridge and continue on the firebreak between the forest and road to Mucklagh Bridge (T 091 857). If you prefer you can continue down the firebreak to join tarmac road at T 096 846, turning right and going downhill on the road for 2km to Mucklagh Bridge. After crossing the bridge, go right, on to a forest road with a barrier. Take the turn hard right at the first junction, then fork right at the next junction higher up and turn left at the T-junction above that and you arrive back at the firebreak you took to head for the summit earlier on.

You can either return to your car the way you came up or turn left on to the other part of the firebreak, walking for about 900m before turning right downhill (A, Sketch 43) and following the Way to reach your car.

Day Five . The Fifth Walk

Aghavannagh to Tinahely

Distance: 26km   *Time*: 6-7 hours

Route Outline   Aghavannagh Hostel – Iron Bridge – Shielstown
Forest Roads – Slievemweel Forest Roads – Slieveroe Boreen –
Ballycumber Old Schoolhouse – Doctor's Monument –
Coolafunshoge Lane – Wooden Bridge – Tinahely.

Parking   Aghavannagh Hostel – Iron Bridge (A, Sketch 46) –
Ballyteigue Bridge (B, Sketch 47) – Moyne Boreen (North end) –
Moyne Boreen (South end) – Ballycumber Forest (North Entrance)
– Ballycumber Forest (South Entrance) – Wooden Bridge (B,
Sketch 61) – Tinahely.

The fifth section of the Wicklow Way soon starts to show contrasts
with all that has gone before. Whereas in previous views bare or
forested hills held the eye, at this point, and from here on, there are
green fields and tillage in every direction.

The hills from here to Clonegal are lower, but highly individual.
They are not part of great groups and ranges, but rise steeply from
small narrow glens, which makes them look higher than they are.

Starting from Aghavannagh Hostel, go back to the Iron Bridge
over the Ow river (Sketch 46); cross this and head up to the hairpin
bend (B, Sketch 46), then go left, after admiring the view NNW to
the South Prison cliffs of Lugnacullia, seen above the forests of
Upper Glen Ow. Next, fork right, entering the forest (D, Sketch
46), and emerging from the trees (A, Sketch 47) close to
Ballyteigue Bridge.

Turn left at A (Sketch 47), cross Ballyteigue Bridge,
immediately turning right to head west on a forest road in the gap.
The Way now goes west on forest roads that use the gap between
Ballygobban Mountain (on the right), and Shielstown Hill (left),
rising to a crossroads (A, Sketch 48) then continuing west to
Junction B, Sketch 48.

There is an impressive glimpse of the South Prison cliffs, beyond

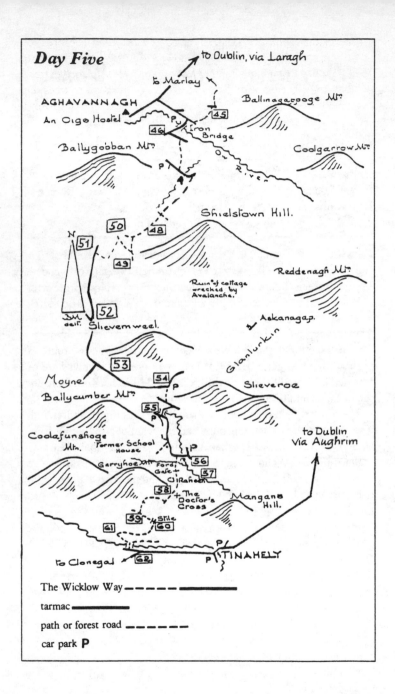

Day Five

to Dublin, via Laragh

to Marlay

AGHAVANNAGH

Ballinagapooge Mtn.

An Oige Hostel

45

46

Iron Bridge

Coolgarrow Mtn.

Ballygobban Mtn.

Ou River

Shielstown Hill.

50

48

Reddenagh Mtn.

N

51

49

Ruins of cottage wrecked by Avalanche.

Askanagap.

BM deit.

52

Glanlurkin

Slievemweel.

53

Moyne

54

P

Slieveroe

Ballycumber Mtn.

55

P

Coolafunshoge Mtn.

Former School House

to Dublin via Aughrim

P

56

Garryhoe Mtn.

Ford; Gate

57

Cllraheen

58

The Doctor's Cross

Mangans Hill.

59

Stile

60

61

P

P TINAHELY

to Clonegal

62

The Wicklow Way ———————

tarmac ━━━━━━

path or forest road — — — — —

car park **P**

the western shoulder of Ballygobban Mountain, before you continue straight (B, Sketch 48); then you follow the forest road south, with a distant view of the Ballycumber Hills framed in trees.

Stay on this road until you emerge from the mature trees and come to a T-junction (A, Sketch 49). Before continuing downhill to the right, pause to gaze at a view extending far beyond the Wicklow Way, to Mount Leinster (Co. Carlow) and Slievenamon (Co. Tipperary), the latter about 100km away, showing that you are now well on the west side of Wicklow.

Walk down this forest road to the next junction (B, Sketch 50) where you turn left. As you descend, Shielstown Hill (536m) is behind you to the east. On the far side of the mountain in a hollow is a ruined farm (T 057 810), the scene of Ireland's only recorded avalanche deaths. It seems that somewhere in the 1860s, a giant snow-slide took place, crushing this house and the family in it (their name was either McCall or Mulhall). A still-living local tradition blames a woman (as usual!) for this tragedy. It is said that a young girl, coming back from mass in Askanagap, threw a snowball at her boyfriend which missed, and started the snow-slide.

On reaching the tarmac road at T 045 825 (A, Sketch 51) you leave forest ground, not entering it again until near the end of today's walk. Now follow about 3kms of road, passing two roads coming in from the right. The second one drops to Moyne Village which has a church and not much else (T 033 802). This place was at one time proposed as the end of the Wicklow Way; hence some of the older timber signposts showed distances to Moyne, not Clonegal.

Look out for Junction A, Sketch 54, where the road bends sharply left and you leave it to the right in favour of an unsurfaced, grass-grown boreen which goes steeply down SW.

The Way rejoins a tarmac road (D, Sketch 55), crosses the stone bridge of Sandyford, and goes up to a T-junction (B, Sketch 55), now complicated by a forest road parallel to the boreen to the left.

But the Way leaves the forest alone, keeping left to the extremely narrow tarmac boreen because the views are better, going SSE and south past the incoming of the same forest road, and on to the former Ballycumber Schoolhouse (A, Sketch 56).

Although it is still shown as a school on several maps, Ballycumber has been a private house for many years. It is your landmark for forking left, after which the road, still tarmac, begins to twist and drop.

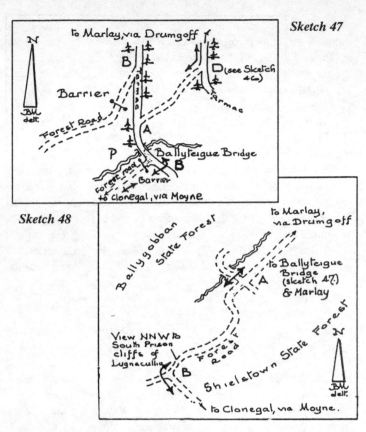

Sketch 47

Sketch 48

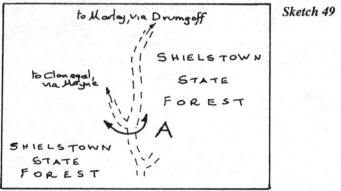

Sketch 49

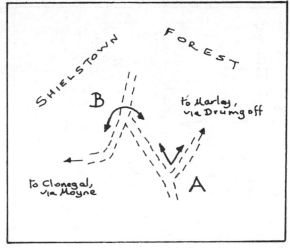

All around there are well-tilled fields, neat new houses, and glimpses SE of Croghan Kinsella or Croghan Mountain (605m), and the highest summit on the Wicklow-Wexford border.

This mountain cradles the Gold Mines River where, in 1797, an Irish version of a gold rush took place, following the discovery of some fair-sized gold nuggets in the river gravels.

Soon, the banks of the Gold Mines River were black with busy prospectors, while indignant landowners protested to the government that, for many miles around, no labourers could be found to save the harvest.

Always sensitive to the needs of property, the government sent troops to put out the private miners, then took over the digging themselves with Mr Thomas Weaver (once a fellow student of the great German scientist and explorer, Alexander Von Humboldt,) as their resident expert. Opponents of state enterprise will note that the expensive government works, in five years after 1798, produced barely £500 worth of fine gold, as opposed to more than £3,000 worth found by local miners in their three weeks' free-for-all.

Traces of Weaver's final effort, a series of narrow opencast workings (technically called 'costeening trenches'), are still to be seen high up on the slopes of Croghan, facing you as you ramble south through Ballycumber. Still locally known as Weaver's

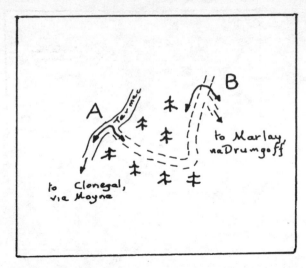

Trenches, these faint lines were an unsuccessful attempt to locate the mother lode.

This is not an area that lays itself out for tourists. You have seen no picnic tables, no forest carparks, since leaving the Iron Bridge, at the start of this day's trek. Motorists seldom visit this area; in fact walkers are about the only tourists ever seen hereabouts. All the more reason then, that walkers here should faithfully follow the country code, especially on the section now just beginning on which there are several gates.

From the former school, the Way goes twisting down to a small stone bridge (C, Sketch 56). Do not cross this bridge, but instead go right, crossing a normally easy ford over a nameless stream that divides the townland of Ballycumber South from that of Ballybeg.

You are now climbing steeply south on a grassy boreen, which levels off only after you pass a second iron gate, beyond which a grassy track continues southerly.

Look out now for three trees ahead, slightly to your right. It is better to steer for these trees by a sheep path to the right (SSW), leaving the main track, which goes close to a stone wall in a hollow which is usually waterlogged (Sketch 57). The trees turn out to be growing on the gapped banks of a ring fort or raheen; there must have been some sort of a dwelling here, perhaps the original 'little homestead', (a literal translation of Ballybeg), probably no more than a timber structure with a stout palisade of timber and thorn

Sketch 52

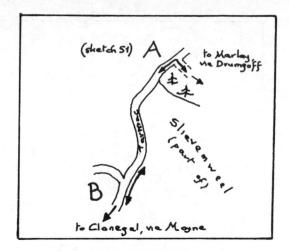

(sketch 51) A
to Marlay, via Drumgoff
Slievemweel (part of)
B
to Clonegal, via Moyne

Sketch 53

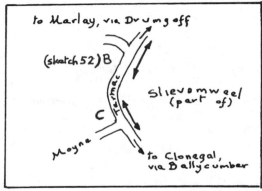

to Marlay, via Drumgoff
(sketch 52) B
Tarmac
C
Slievemweel (part of)
Moyne
to Clonegal, via Ballycumber

Sketch 54

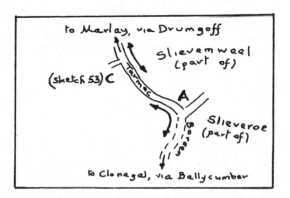

to Marlay, via Drumgoff
Slievemweel (part of)
(sketch 53) C
Tarmac
A
Slieveroe (part of)
to Clonegal, via Ballycumber

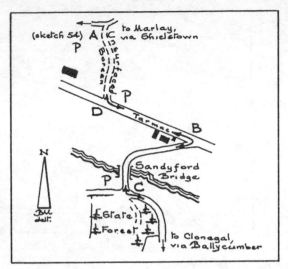

bushes topping the now worn-down banks. As the site has never been scientifically excavated, it is impossible to tell its age or exact usage; it may have been no more than a *buaile* ('booley' on most maps) site – a summer milking-place, where herdsmen lived with their flocks half the year making butter and cheese, a custom which lasted in parts of Wicklow down to the 1880s.

Keep on south by the sheep path which bisects the raheen, and which soon rejoins the main track, now running close to a stone wall. The next landmark comes after the track twists and rises (B, Sketch 58) cutting the corner with a gate in the wall.

Ahead now, built on top of the stone wall on the left, is a small stone cross in memory of a doctor accidentally killed here some seventy years ago when out shooting (A, Sketch 58). The site of this tragedy is a splendid viewpoint. The trail circles the base of Garryhoe Mountain so that, as from a balcony, you look down over the Tinahely area, over the devastated oakwoods of Coolattin, which were ruthlessly exploited despite local and national protests. Above and beyond the varied foreground rise the outlines of Croghan Mountain (606m), and its neighbour, Annagh Hill (454m), both carrying plenty of state forest, and both giving fine ridge walks.

To the left of the northern ridge of Croghan, bearing about ENE, rises a steep, brightly-coloured height which is one of the giant

Sketch 56

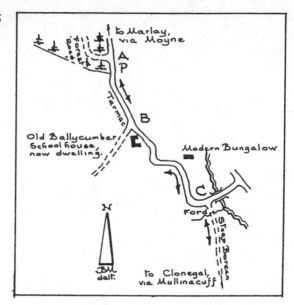

spoil heaps of the unlucky Avoca copper mines, made by Canadian mining interests not long before the mines closed for the last time about 1970 when the world price of copper dropped drastically (T 200 830).

The trail now drops, coming to a crossroads of tracks (B, Sketch 59). You turn right, heading NW towards a small forest in the hollow under Coolafunshoge Mountain.

This track leads into the forest known as Mangan's Wood (C, Sketch 59). Here the track bends east and becomes a forest road, going left again at a T-junction (D, Sketch 60). After another forest gate and stile, you are back on the line of the old track (A, Sketch 60). The next section is Coolafunshoge Lane, an attractive green road with a whole series of fine views, east towards Tinahely and south to Muskeagh Hill, sometimes called 'Four Bounds Hill', because the boundaries of four townlands meet at or near the summit. This lane also has a series of gates. Please leave them exactly as you found them.

Now Junction A (Sketch 61) comes up, where you make a hairpin turn down left; grass on the green road is replaced by gravel and a trace of tarmac. This leads down past a farm, down to a T-junction where on the right you see the ford and old wooden bridge over the Derry River.

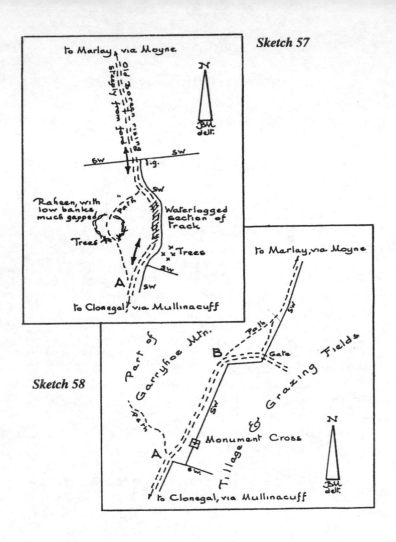

Sketch 57

To Marlay, via Moyne

N

Raheen, with low banks much gapped

Waterlogged section of Track

Trees

x x Trees

A

To Clonegal, via Mullinacuff

Sketch 58

To Marlay, via Moyne

Part of Garryhoe Mtn.

Path

B

Gate

Grazing Fields

Monument Cross

Tillage

A

N

To Clonegal, via Mullinacuff

Cross the bridge here to a full tarmac road, turning left to go SE towards Tinahely village, leaving the Way (C, Sketch 61), for the final 2km into the town, which offers B & B accommodation, plus pubs and shops.

VARIATIONS

Variation One: Shielstown Summit

Distance: 4.5km (extra)   *Time:* 3-3½ hours
(From Aghavannagh Hostel, to make an extra day follow the shorter walk.)

Shielstown Hill (536m), is so close to the track that it is worth a visit. From Ballyteigue Bridge, keep to the Way as far as Junction A, Sketch 48, where you turn left instead of continuing west along the way.

This firebreak is fairly rough, but goes directly to Shielstown summit, which has only a rock outcrop and a small cairn to mark it. Given good visibility, the view here is hard to beat, although some high-level planting now blocks the western sector.

But NNW, you have a matchless panorama of Upper Glen Ow, under the break away of the South Prison cliffs of Lugnacullia, while looking south there is a display of those distinct lower hills that fill the narrow corridor where Wicklow is sandwiched between counties Wexford and Carlow.

Not only the final sections of the Wicklow Way but almost the whole course of the South Leinster Way, from its start below Mount Leinster to its finish in the shadow of Slievenamon, can be seen from Shielstown Hill. Those walking the Wicklow Way will return to the track by their outward route, adding 2km to the day.

If, though, you are staying on in Aghavannagh, you can go down NNW by a ride line that starts just north of the summit, where the forest fence makes a ninety-degree turn. This ride line is broken into giant steps, and is rather wet, being on a north-facing slope. The first road you come to should be taken, to the right, although it curves away around to the SE slopes of Shielstown Hill; the views are worth the detour, as there has been much felling on this side of the hill, opening views across Glen Ow to the sharp peak of Croghan Moira and its neighbours. Make sure to bear left at the first two junctions you meet; the third junction is the crossroads (A, Sketch 48) where you join the Way again.

The crossroads at A is quite close to the northern end of the ride line that led you down from Shielstown summit, but the section between the two forest roads is renowned as a 'demmed, damp, unpleasant' place, where the ride line becomes a morass on the site

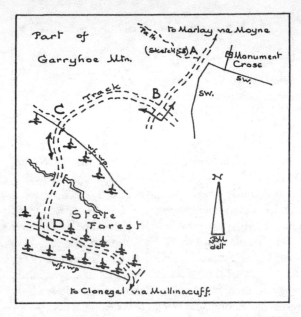

Part of
Garryhoe Mtn.

To Marlay via Moyne

(sketch59) A

Monument
Cross

Track

B

SW.

SW.

C

Track

w.f.w.p

State Forest

D

N

BM
delt

w.f.w.p

To Clonegal via Mullinacuff.

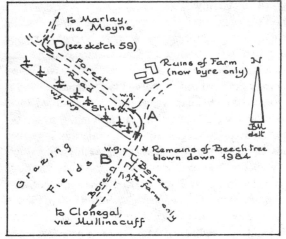

To Marlay,
via Moyne

D (see sketch 59)

Forest Road

Ruins of Farm
(now byre only)

N

w.f.w.p

w.g.

Stile

A

Grazing Fields

B

w.g.

Boreen

* Remains of Beech tree
blown down 1984

Boreen, right to farm only

BM
delt

To Clonegal,
via Mullinacuff

of Percy's Road, shown on some maps, while the drier ground, to
the right, is full of tree stumps and debris from felling.

From the forest crossroads, head back to Aghavannagh Hostel
via the Iron Bridge, as before.

Sketch 61

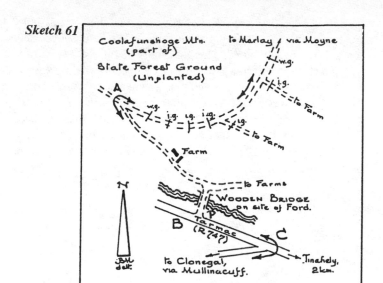

Coolafunshoge Mtn.
(part of)
State Forest Ground
(Unplanted)

to Marlay via Moyne

l.w.g.
i.g.
=to Farm
A
w.g.
i.g. i.g. i.g.
i.g.
=to Farm
Farm
to Farms
WOODEN BRIDGE
on site of Ford.
N
B Tarmac
(R 747)
C
to Clonegal,
via Mullinacuff.
Tinahely,
2 km.
B.M. del.

Variation Two: Coolafunshoge Summit

Distance: same as main route   *Time*: same as main route

Another outstanding viewpoint, quite close to the Way, is Garryhoe
Mountain, with the nearby summit of Coolafunshoge, the latter
carrying a survey pillar since about 1953. Every 'trig station' is, by
definition, a viewpoint, and whenever a small open triangle is
shown on any map, with a height figure in metres or in feet, you
can depend on a good view. But a survey pillar marks a major 'trig
station' from where you have an expansive view, and
Coolafunshoge is no exception.

The detour starts at A, Sketch 59, going up by a path that leads
steadily upwards and which you leave northwards for the last short
climb to the saddle between Garryhoe (397m) and the main
Ballycumber ridge. An old road, probably made for horses and
carts going up to turf cuttings, must have led to a pair of bare and
naked stone piers, once serving a now-vanished gate (T 040 758).
Head slightly left about WNW along the forest fence towards the
trees seen on the western skyline, over mainly dry, slightly broken
ground, slanting a bit left, to your objective, which is at the southern
end of the ridge.

I must admit that I have never had what you might call 'textbook visibility' here, that is, perfect clarity all round the horizon, but I have seen enough to say that as a viewpoint Coolafunshoge takes a lot of beating, although its height is only 431m.

From the survey pillar, start down by heading slightly east of south, till the slope steepens and you see ahead a half-ruined wall, going down SW. Cross this old wall, keeping it on your right hand, turning left when you meet another wall. This will bring you down on to Coolafunshoge Lane, at a wooden gate 400m from the wooden bridge (A, Sketch 61), and the day's distance stays the same.

Shorter Walk – Day Five

1. Shielstown Panorama Point

Distance: 18km from Aghavannagh Hostel or 10km from
Ballyteigue Bridge   *Time*: 7-8 hours from Aghavannagh Hostel
or 3½-4½ hours from Ballyteigue Bridge

Route Outline   Ballyteigue Bridge (B, Sketch 47) – Shielstown
Summit – Ballyteigue Bridge.

Motorists should park at Ballyteigue Bridge (B, Sketch 47). For
those staying in Aghavannagh Hostel, return to Iron Bridge and
keep to the Way as far as Ballyteigue Bridge. Whether you arrive
on foot or by car, from Ballyteigue Bridge follow the Way
(Sketches 47, 48 and 49) as far as A, Sketch 49, to leave it here,
keeping straight on south to where the forest road ends at a gate.
Felling in this area has left the track churned up. Do not cross the
gate, but pause to gaze out across open fields to a view extending
far beyond the Wicklow Way, to Mount Leinster (Co. Carlow) and
Slievenamon (Co. Tipperary), the latter about 100km away.

The next about 150m is covered in debris from felling but it is
possible to pick your way up, keeping the remaining trees on your
right and following the old fence to the grassy ride line you can see
entering the trees above. Emerging at the edge of the trees and
corner of the fence, turn left up the fairly rough forest firebreak.

Twenty minutes or so brings you to the top of Shielstown Hill
(536m) with its small rock outcrop and equally small cairn (T 057
823), while looking south there is a display of those distinct lower
hills that fill the narrow corridor where Wicklow is sandwiched
between Wexford and Carlow. Your descent can be a reversal of
your outward course, making the walk 13km, requiring 4 to 5
hours.

To go down continue along inside the forest fence to a ride line
running NNW and starting where the forest fence makes a
ninety-degree turn. Follow the ride line which is sometimes wet,
being on a north-facing slope. Go straight across the first road you
come to and continue steeply down to a second road below, which
should be taken to the right, although it curves away to the NE
slopes of Shielstown; but the views are worth the detour as there

has been much felling on this side of the hill, opening views across Glen Ow to the sharp peak of Croaghanmoira and its neighbours. Make sure to bear left at the first two junctions you meet; the third junction is the crossroads (A, Sketch 48), where you join the Way again, to get back to where you parked. This crossroads is quite close to the northern end of the ride line that let you down from Shielstown summit, but the section between the two forest roads is a 'demmed, damp, unpleasant place' and blocked by trees growing near the lower end.

For walkers coming from Aghavannagh An Oige Hostel the same route, from the forest crossroads, heads back to the hostel via the Iron Bridge, as before, and their day's journey is 18km.

Day Six . The Sixth Walk

Tinahely to Shillelagh

Distance: 19km   *Time*: 5-6 hours

Route Outline   Tinahely – Muskeagh Boreen – Mullinacuff –
Strankelly Crossroads – Kilquiggin Church and School – Boley
Road Junction – Junction for Raheenakit – Shillelagh.

Parking   Tinahely – Muskeagh Forest Entrance – Mullinacuff Post
Office – Shillelagh.

Start the sixth section of the Way by heading from Tinahely
roughly about NW up the tarmac road R747, signposted for
Hacketstown.

Keeping one eye on the traffic, you look north to Coolafunshoge
Lane and the farm roads below it that have so largely put it out of
business.

Southwards, to the left, is the hollow of Glenphilipeen, under the
Four Bounds Hill, with several boreens which serve farms but do
not link west to the Way.

Sketch 62

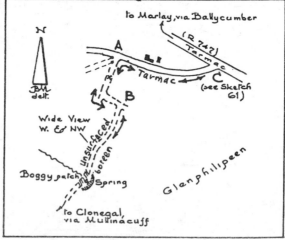

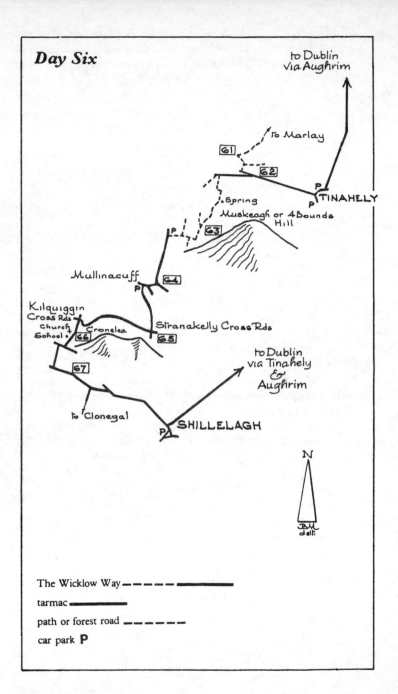

Day Six

to Dublin
via Aughrim

to Marlay

61

62

P
TINAHELY

Spring

Muskeagh or 4 Bounds
Hill

P
63

Mullinacuff

P
64

Kilquiggin
Cross Rds

church

School

66
Cronelea

Stranakelly Cross Rds

65

67

to Dublin
via Tinahely
&
Aughrim

to Clonegal

P
SHILLELAGH

N

BM
delt.

The Wicklow Way — — — —

tarmac —————

path or forest road — — — — —

car park **P**

You rejoin the Wicklow Way (C, Sketch 62) where a tarmac boreen forks steeply up westerly, passing a very small patch of forest on the left (marked on O.S. Sheet 62 1/50000 series as a small green rectangle, at T O19 743), and a neat farm offering B & B on the right. Junction A (Sketch 62) now comes up, a narrow boreen between high banks. At the top of the boreen is a fixed iron gate, after which a left turn, and then right at B (Sketch 62) puts you on to one of the most lovely sections of the Way.

Running narrowly between stone walls, a boreen rises and falls along the western flanks of Four Bounds Hill, keeping roughly to the 230m contour. From this boreen as you head SSW, views open west into Co. Carlow, whose boundary is here barely 4km away, across the isolated Seskin Hill.

There is a fine clear spring on your left, flowing strongly most times, and its overflow often makes the trail muddy, but it is a small obstacle, soon passed. The site of this spring is of special significance for all Wicklow Way walkers, because it stands just over 100km from Marlay Park, so a halt and some congratulations are called for here. The boreen twists and rises now past the shell of a ruined farm, marked as a sound, well-roofed house on the 6 inch plan of 1910, though you would be pardoned for thinking that those gaunt, gapped walls were relics of the 1847 Famine, or of an

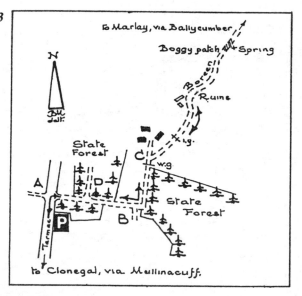

Sketch 63

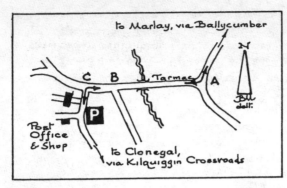

Sketch 64

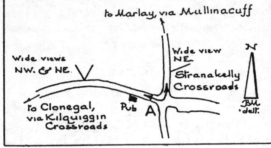

Sketch 65

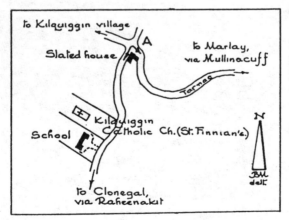

Sketch 66

108

Sketch 67

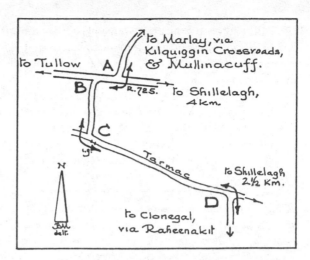

To Marlay, via
Kilquiggin Crossroads,
& Mullinacuff.

To Tullow A

B R.725. To Shillelagh,
4 km.

C

Tarmac

To Shillelagh
2½ km.

N

D

To Clonegal,
via Raheenakit

earlier time. A working farm is passed on the right, and after a wooden gate, state forest comes in on the left, while the boreen surface becomes rather more like that of a regular road, especially after you turn right and go downhill (B, Sketch 63).

You meet a tarmac road at a T-junction, and go left (signposts are high on the right bank; large trailers are often parked on the left). You are heading SSW, and the first landmark is a junction on a curve, at A, Sketch 64, where you go right to reach Mullinacuff village. Take the second turn left there, the road for Stranakelly crossroads (C, Sketch 64).

You are now on the upper of two roads built very close together, and both leading SSE (S 991 724). Usually the road higher on a hill is the older of the two, while a road on an easier grade is often more recent, perhaps a famine relief road (from the 1840s), built on the principle that starving men must do a day's work before getting any help – though I have heard nothing about these twin roads in local tradition. At Stranakelly crossroads turn right, and at once begin a stiff climb westward over the lower shoulders of Cronelea Hill (357m), another of these hills divided among townlands, in this case, Ballymarroge, Cronelea, Stranakelly and Ballynultagh. You look over much of eastern Co. Carlow, back towards the Hump of Hacketstown and the hills you have traversed; then comes a short downhill stretch to a bridge over a stream, followed by a rise to Kilquiggin crossroads (A, Sketch 66).

Next, the Way leaves the modern schoolhouse and St Finnian's

Catholic church on the right, thus bypassing the main part of Kilquiggin village, which is off to the NW at the tail of Seskin Hill. Continue SW, downhill, coming to the T-junction where the Way meets the main Tullow-Shillelagh road, (R725) at A and B (Sketch 67). This is a skewed crossroads, shown as a straight-through cross on older maps which is a fairly sure sign that a serious road accident once happened here and that the crossroads was staggered to prevent a repeat, but I haven't met any local person to check my theory. A short uphill follows, after leaving the main road (at B, Sketch 67), as you make for a T-junction.

A Wicklow Way signpost marks the junction (C, Sketch 67) and is on the right as you come up the hill. Now you start the final section of the Way for day six – a fairly level easterly stretch at about 180m where, on the right, you look south to rising ground with forests which is part of Stookeen Mountain, almost the last barrier between you and Clonegal.

You leave the Way at D (Sketch 67) because Shillelagh town is still slightly more than 2km ahead, continuing straight on east to join the main road R725, where you bear right.

This road loses height pretty steadily and you have to turn right finally, to drop down into the town. Shillelagh is more compactly built than Tinahely; it was once the terminus of a branch railway and it has the unmistakable stamp of an estate village. It was once owned by the Earls Fitzwilliam, whose mansion, Coolattin, is about 2km east of the town. There is B & B accommodation available, and after booking in you can stroll down to the bridge over the Derry River, which you first saw as a stripling stream at the old wooden bridge above Tinahely.

VARIATIONS

Variation One: Via Cross Bridge

Distance: same as main route   *Time*: same as main route

As the Wicklow Way uses almost all the surviving tracks and high level roads, a change of route hereabouts is not always an improvement. But if, after setting out from Tinahely, you find you have forgotten to make a telephone call – don't despair! Instead, keep straight on at junction C (Sketch 62) and again straight on at

B (Sketch 61) where the old wooden bridge leads to Coolafunshoge Lane. This brings you to an imposing fork in the tarmac road. You go left, and left again if you wish, passing the Bridgelands Catholic church; either of these left forks will bring you to a fork in the road and a card telephone box at Cross Bridge. The variation route passes the telephone box, taking the left fork to a junction (T 003 747) where you go left again, joining the Way at A (Sketch 63).

Variation Two: Mullinacuff to Kilquiggin crossroads (direct route)

Distance: 2.5km less   *Time*: 1 hour less

This low-level variation starts at Mullinacuff village where, instead of turning left for Stranakelly crossroads (Sketches 64 and 65), you go straight ahead, passing on your left a Church of Ireland church, before coming to a junction (S 988 726) and turning left. This Mullinacuff road gives long-range views of the hills, and meets the Way at Kilquiggin crossroads (A, Sketch 66), saving 2km over the official route.

Shorter Walk – *Day Six*

A Taste of the South

Distance: 7.25km   *Time*: 2-2½ hours

Park at the forest boreen (A, Sketch 63) and follow the Wicklow Way in reverse, heading toward Marlay Park (Sketches 63, 62). This lets you enjoy the wide views west and NW from the lofty boreen on the flanks of Muskeagh or 'Four Bounds' Hill, and there are impressive views north also, to the steep slopes of Coolafunshoge, rising like a wall ahead. You meet a tarmac road (A, Sketch 62) and go left, towards Bridgelands Catholic church. Take each left turn that you meet – this will have you circling back to your car, with the hills previously traversed now on your left.

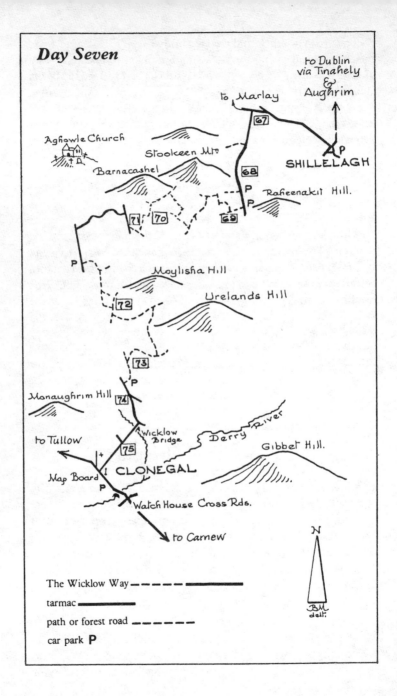

Day Seven

to Dublin
via Tinahely
&
Aughrim

to Marlay

67

Aghowle Church

Stookeen Mtn.

Barnacashel

68

P

SHILLELAGH

P

Raheenakit Hill.

71   70

69

P

P

Moylisha Hill

Urelands Hill

72

73

P

Monaughrim Hill

74

Wicklow
Bridge

Derry River

Gibbet Hill.

to Tullow

75

CLONEGAL

Map Board

P

Watch House Cross Rds.

to Carnew

N

The Wicklow Way ─ ─ ─ ─ ═══

tarmac ═══════

path or forest road ─ ─ ─ ─

car park **P**

BM
delt.

112

Day Seven . *The Seventh Walk*

Shillelagh to Clonegal

Distance: 22km   *Time*: 6-7 hours

Route Outline   Shillelagh – Tullow Road – Boley Junction – Raheenakit Road – Raheenakit forest – Boreen in Aghowle Upper – Moylisha Boreen – Moylisha Forest – Newry Forest – Wicklow Bridge – Clonegal.

Parking Shillelagh – Raheenakit First Forest Entrance (B, Sketch 68) – Raheenakitt Second Forest Entrance (C, Sketch 68) – Moylisha Forest Entrance (A, Sketch 72) – Urelands Forest Entrance (A, Sketch 73) – Clonegal.

Your final section of the Wicklow Way begins with a 3km tarmac stretch, from Shillelagh by the Tullow road, and thus back to the official line of the Way at Junction D, Sketch 68. The road up from Shillelagh runs between hills, with state forest to the left, on the eastern extension of Raheenakit townland.

The landmark to watch for is a pair of gate piers, on the right, which warns you not to miss the fork left for Boley townland (S 966 695). These gate piers have their own interest, too; they mark the southern end of what looks very like an old road (you passed the northern end of it, close to Kilquiggin, Sketch 66). As so often happened in the eighteenth and nineteenth centuries, this older road may have been taken into a demesne and closed to ordinary traffic; hence the gate piers.

From the main road fork you rise to the junction in Boley townland (D, Sketch 68), and turn left to head south there.

This road is another of the surprises of the Wicklow Way. It begins with barely a hint of mountainy ground, bringing you past green fields, past a neat farm on the left, with a great display of hydrangeas, and past another farm, also on the left, after which the whole scene changes. After you cross a small stone bridge, there begins one of the steepest climbs on any public road in Wicklow, set at about 1 in 12 at first, increasing to 1 in 7 near the crest. Wide

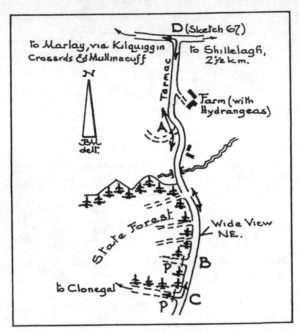

Sketch 68

views open behind you to NNE, showing the line you have already followed, while the views west, though open now, were blocked by forest planted between 1950 and 1960 until it was felled in the last few years and replanted.

You pass a forest entrance on the right (B, Sketch 68), keep on to just over the crest of the hill, and turn right there at a second forest entrance with a gate and barrier and forest on the right hand only (C, Sketch 68). You now realise that you are on a fair height. The open ground on the left gives southerly views to Gibbet Hill, 315m (S 946 593), inside the Wexford border, seen across the glen of the Derry River flowing west to join the River Slaney.

Despite this fine view, don't miss a turn right at A (Sketch 69) because if you do you will end up on the wrong side of the forest and well off the Wicklow Way. But the Way, from Junction A, curves away west, before you make two right angle turns – D (Sketch 69) then left at E (Sketch 70).

This brings you past side turn F (Sketch 69) to a Coillte notice, warning you of a change in the line of the Way at Junction G (Sketch 69), where you go right. You turn right and then left with the road and on to a T-junction. Going left puts you onto a

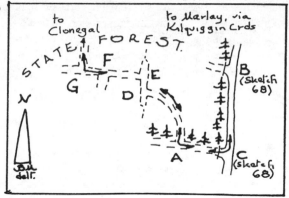

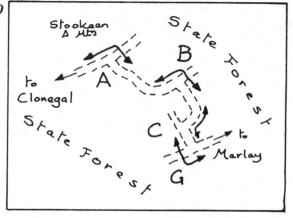

nicely-curving west and SW line to another junction where you go left again. After a short distance the trees stop on the left of the road and you are close under Stookeen Mountain on your right. At 420m, this is the last 400m point near the Way, but although Stookeen is well supplied with forest roads, it is something of a grind to reach the top because of extra deep heather, with furze lower down.

I have seen deer on this mountain, mostly Sika and Sika/Red deer crossbreeds. They were a long way from the reputed origin of the wild Sika of the Powerscourt demesne, whence they escaped, it is believed, through the damaged Watergates (Sketch 15) back in the 1920s. I feel that other park herds must have contributed to the Sika population, which now exists far beyond the borders of Leinster.

Meanwhile the Way brings you to a firebreak dropping steeply left where the trees start again (C, Sketch 71). You descend the firebreak, with these trees now on your right, as it bends right and then left to leave you on a boreen – and at the end of the change in the line of the Way. This boreen brings you westerly on an improving surface and past a cottage. The SSW views widen to include Mount Leinster, with its TV mast, and the nearer, forested hills of Newry and Urelands, the last barrier between you and Clonegal.

The boreen meets a tarmac road shortly after passing the cottage (Sketch 71). Bear right on reaching the road (D, Sketch 71) heading NW for some 800m over the crest of a rise till, just where a descent begins, you go left (B, Sketch 71), on what an auctioneer would surely describe as 'a boreen of character', which twists, turns, rises and falls, in a bewildering manner. It is almost as if the Wicklow Way, here so near its end, was determined to give you as many memorable moments as possible, for there are extensive views back north towards 'Lug', as well as a view back NE to Barnacashel, the unplanted western shoulder of Stookeen Mountain (420m, not named on O.S. Sheet 62 1/50000).

Locally called 'the Churches', this hill carries quite an array of early sites, raheens, mounds and cairns, all more or less battered. Nearer to the twisting boreen is a cromlech or dolmen called Lobnasye, or Moylisha dolmen in the official list of National Monuments (S 930 680). This prehistoric tomb is not visible from the

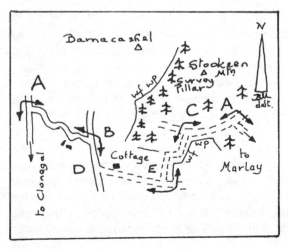

Sketch 71

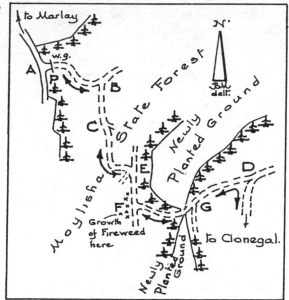

Way, and is hard to reach, being in farmland with no access track, and with several fences to cross. The site has been excavated, and is reckoned to date from 1000 B.C. at least.

The boreen straightens at last, coming to a T-junction, at A, Sketch 71.

Turn left here to follow a straight road south, dull by comparison with what you have just traversed, until you come alongside forest again on the left, after about a kilometre. Then you get variety a-plenty. You go in by the forest entrance, on the left, opposite a field gate from which one clear evening I saw Slievenamon Mountain, the best part of 100km away, etched clearly on the horizon.

Inside the forest entrance (A, Sketch 72) the road twists and rises slightly to junction B, where the Way turns right to lead you south and a little east, along a level, straight and normally little-used forest road, grass-grown in the centre, except where thinning of trees has churned some of it up. Ornamental *Cupressus* are on the right – a tree seldom planted in state forests.

Past junction C (Sketch 72), with a grassy bank, the Way curves east to a T-junction (E, Sketch 72), turning south again where the forest road passes a large colony of fireweed, their purple flowers, in season, making an agreeable contrast with the usual dark green of the forest.

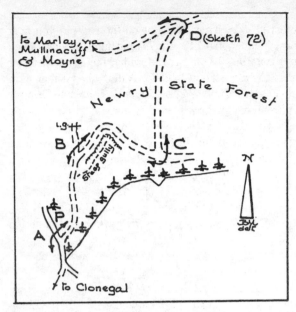

Sketch 73

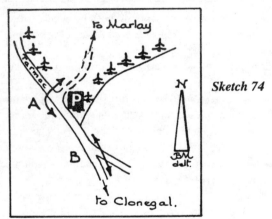

Sketch 74

Then go left at F (Sketch 72) as you come to a short neck of recently-planted ground between Moylisha Forest, now behind you, and the Newry Forest ahead and above you.

There is a fairly steep rise before you, to junction D (Sketch 73). This is a somewhat distorted T-junction, where a sweeping turn right is made to start the final long southern slant that the Way makes in forest ground. Trees thin out on the right as you near makes in forest ground. Trees thin out on the right as you near another curving T-junction (C, Sketch 73) and there are views away SW to Mount Leinster, 793m, around which the South Leinster Way runs, a trail whose start at Kildavin Village is less than 4km from the end of the Wicklow Way at Clonegal. The South Leinster and the Wicklow Ways are both part of the national network being set up by the National Waymarked Ways Committee. Now you go down sharply to the right, heading NW from junction C, past an odd, slightly swampy gully on the left; this may be no more than a gravel pit, from which material for the forest roads was taken, but with traces of a road up the middle of it. At B (Sketch 73) the Way goes left, on what was once the main drive up to Urelands House, now a forest road leading you south to the last forest gate on the Way (A, Sketch 74). Fork right (B, Sketch 74) to go down to the final T-junction leading to Wicklow Bridge, where you enter Co. Carlow (B, Sketch 75).

The final fairly straight section of the Way leads SSW, ignoring junction (A, Sketch 75). For about 2.5km you walk with the Derry River fairly close by on the left, and always the forests of Gibbet Hill, seen beyond the river.

Journey's end is now close, as you come in sight of Clonegal, with its two churches and village green, on which you will find a

Sketch 75

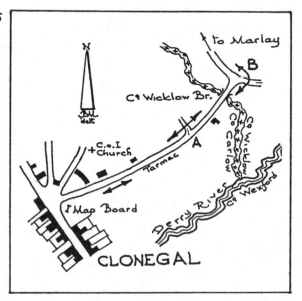

119

map board displaying the whole route back to the gates of Marlay Park.

In Clonegal you meet the Derry River once again, last seen if you strolled down to the bridge in Shillelagh, and now crossed by a fine bridge, the last before it joins the Slaney. Huntington Castle (which, since about 1975, has become a centre for reviving the worship of Isis) is open to the public at certain times between May and September. Down the street, to the left at – and on the other side of the road from – the map board as you come to the end of the Way, is a pub without a trace of plastic.

VARIATIONS

Variation One: Barnacashel and Stookeen Summits

Distance: 5km (extra) *Time*: 2 hours (extra)

Inveterate peak-baggers will not pass near a prominent summit like Stookeen, 420m, without attempting the top, and its interesting western neighbour, Barnacashel, which has a variety of antiquities.

For Stookeen Mountain, leave the Way at B (Sketch 69) to follow a forest road west, passing a road to the right and climbing gradually to just over 300m to a T-junction. Going right, look out for a ride line which has become a road going up diagonally left, and its continuation, less clear, going down to the right (S 953 681). This is where you turn up left, heading about NW.

Continue up this road/ride line, going straight all the way up to about 360m, after which comes a steep descent straight to a small enclosure (a house site) and directly opposite along a narrow banked boreen to leave forest ground at S 945 687. You step out on pleasant open ground on a southern extension of Barnacashel Hill, not named on the maps, but now in Aghowle Lower townland (many townland boundaries were 'tidied-up' by the original Ordnance Survey, about 1830, and names of many townlands, still locally known to this day, were never officially recorded). Head just south of west across the open ground for the top of the southern extension.

Barnacashel is locally called The Churches, and is associated with the legend of St Finden (a local saint, probably seventh century), who had a hermitage here till a miraculous wind carried off his cloak, which came to earth at the site of the present ruined church in Aghowle Lower.

Retrace your steps back into the forest to the small enclosure and turn right on to the forest road. This road rises as it circles around Stookeen Mountain heading SW and then south. Where the trees thin on your left to a single line of larch alongside the road you have the option to head for the top of Stookeen, climbing steeply just over 300m up the rough ground, clear of trees, to the summit with its survey pillar.

Mount Leinster dominates the southern view, but Lugnacullia still looks impressive northwards though almost 25km away, which is as far from the mountain southward as Djouce is to the NE.

You should return by the same route to the road and then turn left to continue on southwards to join a road coming in from the right and meet the Way where it turns steeply down the firebreak (C, Sketch 71) with trees on your right and fields on your left.

Variation Two: Alternative via Crab Lane Crossroads

Distance: 22km (alternative to main Day Seven route)
Time: 7-8 hours

Another variation caters for those who prefer wide views and curious antiquities to forest trails and less tarmac. Start from Shillelagh to link up with the Way at D (Sketch 68), as before, but this time keep straight on west, backtracking to Junction C (Sketch 67). Continue west, instead of turning downhill to the staggered crossroads at R725. This brings you over to Coolkenna Street, a hillside village set at about 150m, giving views between NW and NE towards Co. Carlow and to Kilquiggin, seen across a broad glen.

Turn left uphill at Coolkenna, passing the Church of Ireland church on left, then about 270m further on you come to the remains of an odd landmark 'The Six Trees' (S 942 709). Though barely one tree and a stump now survive, they are still marked on the Six Inch plans, and there were four in place when I first saw them in the 1950s. Possibly a landlord's joke, there were originally three on each side of the road, almost like a barricade, 'leaving barely room for one cart to pass', according to the 'Ordnance Survey Name Books', about 1825.

Your next landmark is Crab Lane crossroads, really a T-junction, where you go left again, and almost at once the road begins to rise and twists south once more.

There is a pub (on the right) at this crossroads, a convenient place to halt and perhaps celebrate the fact that you have almost completed half your circuit round Stookeen summit, but another interesting landmark lies ahead. Aghowle Church (S 932 694) is a National Monument, built upon a prominent mound, on the traditional site on which St Finden's cloak came to earth.

You reach the church by a straight boreen, that goes diagonally down to the right, from a tarmac road, and then climb a stile to get into the graveyard.

Aghowle Church (which dates from the twelfth century) has a small highly decorated window in the east wall, and an impressive west doorway with slanted jambs, perhaps from Syrian or Egyptian influence (the Celtic monks had many links with the Middle East).

Inside the east wall, there is a deep square recess, which is 'the Mill of Purgatory'. What you do is, get your head and shoulders into this recess, and at once you will hear a steady, low-pitched rumbling sound – this is the rumble of the Mill of Purgatory, at which the soul of the last person buried in the graveyard has to toil, till relieved by the next soul to arrive from Aghowle. What will happen when the Minister finally makes an order, closing this ancient graveyard, the legends do not say!

Now it is back to a tarmac road. Keep on southerly, on a rising road, to put Barnacashel summit steadily behind you.

Thus you come back to the Wicklow Way at Junction B (Sketch 71) and follow the official route by Moylisha Forest, into Clonegal.

Shorter Walk – *Day Seven*

Final Forest Circuit

Distance: 4km *Time*: 1½-2 hours

Urelands Hill is the final forest traversed by the Wicklow Way, before reaching the trail's end in Clonegal, but it is well worth a visit for its own sake.

Motorised walkers park at A (Sketch 73) then follow the Way back by junctions B and C, as far as Junction D (Sketch 73).

From this angle of approach, this is a T-junction, and here you leave the Way and follow the forest road system right around the hill, running pretty level all the way and very close to the eastern edge of the forest where the felling and replanting work which has been carried out gives clear views towards Stookeen Mountain and over the Shillelagh countryside, before you come back around to extra-wide Junction C (Sketch 73) and retrace your steps to your parked car.

Index

Tibradden Mountain 44
Roundwood 58, 63
Rucksack 18

S

Scarr Mountain 71
Schoolpaths 68
Seskin Hill 107
Seven churches, Glendalough 68
Shielstown Hill 84, 89, 99, 103-104
Shillelagh 110, 113
Shop River, bus terminus 47, 49
Sika deer 15-16
Sinn Féin 81
Six Trees 121
Slazenger (Powerscourt) Estate 52
Sleamaine 57
Slieve Margy, Co. Carlow 82
Slievemweel 89
Slievenamon, Co. Tipperary 99,
   103, 117
Slieveroe boreen 89
South gate, Marlay Park 33
South Leinster Way 99, 119
South Prison Cliffs, Lugnacullia 84, 89
South Ring Highway, Dublin 33
St Finden's cloak, legend of 120
St Finnian's Church, Kilquiggin 109
St John's Church, Laragh 70
St Saviour's Church, Glendalough 68,
   73
Stoney Road Glenmalure 75, 86
Stookeen Mountain 110, 115,
   120-121, 123
Stranakelly crossroads 109
Strongbow's march, route of 23
Survey pillars
   Croaghanmoira Mountain 82, 87-88,
   99, 104
   Djouce Mountain 40, 49, 51, 54, 56,
   59, 82, 121
   Prince William Seat 44

Stookeen Mountain 110, 115-116,
   120-123
Synge, J.M. 43, 69

T

Three Stones of Djouce 59
Tibradden Mountain 44
Ticknock Forest Car Park 46
   Forest road 36
   Rifle Range 45
Tiglin National Adventure Centre 20
Tinahely 97
Tonduff Mountain 40, 47, 60
Tonelagee Mountain 17, 57, 66
Torch 19
Trooperstown Hill (Mweeleen) 64, 70
Trotter, J. B., *Walks in Ireland, 1812*
   23
'Tunnel of Love' 78

U

Upper Lough, Glendalough 74
Urelands Hill 122
   House 119

V

Vallency, General 60
Van Dieman's Mines, Glendalough 68
Vandalism 14, 52
Vartry reservoirs 63

W

Walkers without maps 23
Walking 'Don'ts 19
Walks in Ireland, 1812, J. B. Trotter 23
Whistle 20
Whitechurch Bridge 33
Wicklow Bridge 119
Wicklow National Park 53
Wicklow Way
   Marking System 13
   Origins of 13
Woollen Mills, the 73